You Can Go to College for FREE!

Rhea M. Watson

The Scholarship Doctor

Mrs. Trina —

I hope this book is a blessing to you and your family for many generations.

Love,

You Can Go to College for FREE!

Copyright © 2023 by Rhea M. Watson

The Traveling Toddler Publishing Company

Printed in the United States of America

All rights reserved

ISBN: 978-1-7356243-3-4

This publication is mostly based on personal, educational, and entrepreneurial experiences and testimonials of authors, clients and/or others. The author /publisher has made every effort to ensure that the information in this book is true and accurate. This publication is to provide accurate information regarding the subjects covered, the author/publisher assumes no responsibilities for errors, inaccuracies, omissions, or other incorrect information herein and hereby displaying any liability to any party for any laws, damages, or disruptions caused by errors or omissions, whether purposed or otherwise.

The author/publisher does not claim, nor should the reader assume that any individual experience is typical or representative of what any other consumers might experience. There is no promise of scholarships, grade increases, test score increases, free college, free tuition, or any monetary or in-kind compensation.

Please consult a professional college/scholarship consultant to assist in your scholarship and college needs.

Any trademarks, service marks, product name, or named features are assumed to be the property of their respective owners and are used only reference. There is no implied endorsement if the authors/publisher used one of the terms.

myscholarshipsolutions.com

702.623.9500 (office)

Dedication

We dedicate this book to our friends, family, followers, and fans.

We pray that these inspired chapters will help us fill the mission to see 1 Million Scholars, yes you are a scholar, to attend college for FREE!

Please read each chapter, and implement the keys, nuggets, and suggestions.

We believe in you and want you to go for every dream.

Table of Contents

Introduction
By: Rhea M. Watson 2

Free Money! Five Easy Ways You Can Go to College for FREE!
By: Rhea M. Watson 6

Veterans Benefits Matter
By: Lili St. Christopher 14

Family Matters
By: Marilyn Gilbert-Mitchell 20

College Prep Exams can save you MONEY!
By: Shymika Stephenson-Davison 28

The Hidden Costs of Losing a Full Scholarship
By: Carol Ben-Davies 34

Four Keys to Keep You Going to College For Free Once You Get There
By: Nathan McCalla 40

Application Salvation: The First Stepping Stone to Your College Career
By: Nikayla Williams 46

Supporting The Dream: From Community to Campus With Love *By: Zena Robinson-Wouadjou and Vanessa Emile | SchoolWideRead* 52

Standing Up and Stepping Out
By: Sydnie Chandler Monet' Collins 58

Sticks and Stones
By: Orrick R. Quick Sr 64

A Scholarship Would Have Made a World of Difference: The Faith of an International Student
By: Joseph Boumah 70

Changing a Legacy
By: Racquel Watson Boumah 74

The 5 Sweet Nuggets to Applying for Scholarships

By: Justyn D. Boumah..	80
Scholarships..	84
Thanks and Tips..	92
Rhea's Resources	98

"You can go to college for free and you should!"
Rhea M. Watson
The Scholarship Doctor

Introduction

By: Rhea M. Watson

It all started with this simple direct message, "I have a God Idea. I want to bring extraordinary minds together to share how we help students to go to college for free. Would you like to write with me?"

I thought about it, prayed about it, and invited professionals in the field of college readiness to hear my vision and 12 of the most brilliant and blessed human beings answered the call and created, what I believe to be the first of its kind, a periodical of voices who will show you and yours what is possible, plausible, and paramount in regard to securing a free college education.

My Daddy used to say, "Free ain't always FREE!" I can attest that this is the case when it comes to the college scholarship/tuition space. To get free money you have to work for it, you have to want it, and you have to be willing. Willing to do what you may ask? Mostly, not to give up on yourself. I and many of the collaborating authors in this book have the privilege of working with students and families, directing them so they can get into college, eliminate student loans, earn college scholarships, maintain their mental health, stay encouraged, stay in college, learn how to best rely on and use family, college, and community resources, and more. Although we provide expert advice, assistance, advocacy, and accountability, students and families have to receive the information provided, then implement, follow up and follow through. Providing tools, tips, techniques, tricks, and tactics are great! However, if students' receptors are blocked and they are unwilling to do the work of submitting applications, tuning into tutoring and test prep, monitoring relationships with mentors, or managing their mental health, a free education will be nearly impossible to obtain.

Therefore, I strongly encourage you to start at the first chapter of this book and read everything from cover to cover. Taking time to digest the information will provide you with jewels so that you can see success. Also, going to college for free is available to students, we call you scholars, of all ages. Whether you are an elementary, middle, high school or a college/ university student, there is phenomenal, life changing information in this book that will be superbly beneficial to you.

Colleagues, Professionals, Parents, Educators, Mentors, Ministers, and Community Activists, we need you to use your influence with kids, teens, and adults by sharing the importance of this book. Your leadership will "lead the ship" and its passengers. Therefore, please use this book as a classroom resource, add it to your school or public library, have it serve as a summer project, turn to it for a student or parent Bible study, or have it to be at the helm of your community book club. Assuring that your community has this book as a walking stick down the path to college and scholarship success will help us to end the tragic narratives associated with the student loan debt crisis and completely change the messages to read that You and Yours Can go to College for FREE - and the terrific text in your hands is a guide to that freedom!

The title of this book is simple, "You Can Go to College for Free!" and it is undoubtedly, absolutely possible. Personally, I have testimony after testimony of students and parents who pay ZERO Dollars for their or their children's college education. In fact, about 70% of my clients are on salary for attending college. However, these incredible statistics do not come from wishing and hoping but rather planning, preparing, practicing, yes praying, and following the path established by a professional expert in the field of college and scholarship readiness. Amazingly, in this book, you have over a dozen experts who are opening the vault so that you can see and know how to go to college for free.

My collaborating authors and I respect your commitment, your sacrifices, and your bravery. We know you have to take the road less traveled to firstly, attend college, and secondly, especially, to do so without using student loans. We are confident that this book is a game changer, a life changer, for our blessed readers. We know you can do this! We really do believe in you and the power you have to make monumental strides in your college and scholarship journeys. We want to celebrate your successes, wins, and developed wisdom. We invite you to share the nuggets you receive from the chapters and the roadmap you have created because of the priceless information you received from the book. Furthermore, we urge you to share the book with others. You Can Go to College for FREE! is a fantastic gift for birthdays, bar mitzvah/bat mitzvah, baby showers, and bon voyages (graduation or going away parties). Honestly, one of the greatest gifts you can give someone is freedom, and this book serves as a subject matter leader for going to college debt free.

The contact information for all of the authors is listed with their chapters. Please follow, share, and reach out to us. We want to join in your joy. Thank you for being a part of our college and scholarship community. Your support is noticed, important, and deeply appreciated.

Many Blessings and Thanks!

Rhea M. Watson
The Scholarship Doctor
Scholarship Solutions, LLC
myscholarshipsolutions.com
@scholarshipdr
702.623.9500 (o)

You Can Go to College for FREE!

Rhea M. Watson
The Scholarship Doctor
Founder/CEO of Scholarship Solutions

Rhea M. Watson, Scholarship Doctor and Founder/CEO of Scholarship Solutions, a Premier Scholarship and College Consulting Firm, is dedicated to working with students worldwide ages 0 to 99. As an international speaker, Rhea has presented to audiences in Egypt, England, France, Germany, Gabon, India, Jamaica, Japan, Libya, Mexico, Nigeria, Portugal, South Africa, Spain, and all across the United States of America, teaching students of all ages how to have a debt free college experience.

Rhea has assisted hundreds of students to enter the colleges of their dreams and win more than $200 Million Dollars in scholarships. She has received numerous honors, including Community Partnership Award, HBCU for Life Award, Highest GPA Honor, and US-Africa International Women's Day Award. Rhea has been featured on the TODAY show, Good Morning America, and in Forbes and Black Enterprise Magazines. She is the #1 best selling author of The Scholarship Doctor is in! 5 Easy Steps to a FREE Degree.

myscholarshipsolutions.com
@scholarshipdr on Tik Tok, IG, FB, Clubhouse, Twitter, LinkedIn, and YouTube

Free Money!

Five Easy Ways You Can Go to College for FREE!
By: Rhea M. Watson

It had been clearly explained that the red light was my indicator to go. I had practiced thoroughly, memorized each line and every step, and felt undoubtedly prepared to introduce myself and my God Idea to an army of unknown professionals and investors. Sweaty palms, a beaming smile, and the confidence of a toddler as they jump into the arms of their daddy with unbarred faith confident, they will be caught midair, I believed this was my time to win! Red light on - My pitch began and in three minutes with pure grit, unharbored emotion, and sincere dedication I left it all on the table. My three minutes of fame turned into $10,000 in cash! They loved my idea! They believed in my concept and out of 1000 applicants they chose me!

I could share story after story regarding my own winning experiences as well as the triumphant wins of hundreds of my clients from ages 0 - 90. These individuals have taken humongous leaps of faith by sharing their God Ideas, personal stories of heroism, dissertations on grief and injustice, and comical creative tales and poems. Collectively, at a podium, by uploading a video, or pushing submit on an online application, we have forged a path to a life of debt freedom for educational and entrepreneurial endeavors.

The fortitude needed to secure debt freedom, especially to go to college, has been mostly relegated to scholarships. Yes! Scholarships are surely a great way to pay for college and this funding source as well as fellowships, which are scholarships for graduate students, have been an incredibly important resource in my academic journey. However, I have used, learned about, and shared multiple financial opportunities and options.

Excitedly, there are several avenues where you can use OPM (other people's money) to attend college, therefore you can avoid using your own financial resources like household budget, household savings, or college savings. Many of these less-traveled pathways have helped my clients and me reach the ultimate goal of going to college for free. Let's break down scholarships and a few other ways that you can use to pay college tuition, room and board, and other expenses regarding college costs.

When it comes to going to college debt, free scholarships, seemingly, are the first thing that comes to mind or a part of the discussion. Sometimes people will mention grants or loans thinking that those are surefire ways to pay for a college education. So, what is a scholarship? A scholarship is free money from a college or business that does not have to be paid back. Here is a list of my top Must apply for scholarships:

Scholarships

- Get Educated Online Scholarships - College Students Studying Online
- American Veterans AMVets Scholarships - Kindergarten - 12th Grades
- Heisman High School Scholarship - Graduating High School Seniors

- Patriot's Pen Scholarship - 6th - 8th Grades
- Visionary Scholarship 9th - 12th Grades

From my early years as a doctoral student until the present, I have competed in elevator, business plan, and business pitch competitions and I have won 10s of 1000s of dollars. I also have clients, as young as age five, who have competed and won money pitching! Practically every day you can find a competition for children, teens, and adults. The traditional process with pitch competitions is the presentation of a concept or concrete business, idea, product, or vision. In 60 seconds - three minutes you share your business or product with judges. Pitches can occur live in person, live through a video platform, pre-recorded in some shape or fashion, or perhaps as a written or photographic montage. Most times these competitions are completely free of charge to enter but can produce huge financial rewards! Check out these fantastic pitch competitions in which the whole family can participate.

Pitch Competitions

- Rice University Student Business Plan Competition - Prizes $5,000 - $350,000
- World Youth Entrepreneurship Challenge Ages 11-18 - Prizes $1,000 - $5,000
- Diamond Challenge for High School Students - Prizes $4,000 - $12,000
- Y Combinator Demo Day for Startup Entrepreneurs - Prizes $500,000

- National Black Business Pitch Competition - Prizes $2,500 - $10,000

Have you ever heard of mystery shoppers? Have you ever received a phone call or text message asking you to provide your opinion in exchange for a sum of money? Well, these activities are great ways to subsidize your college tuition costs, business, or personal income. See, since my undergraduate days I have participated in focus groups. Focus groups are created by research, medical, or marketing companies that need and want your feedback on a particular product or service. Because you provide them with important information, they pay you for those details. Here are a few of the best businesses where you can participate in focus groups.

Focus Groups

- V & L Research and Consulting, Inc - Looking for BIPOC and other niche groups
- Respondent - Get paid by participating in college research lab opportunities
- Fieldwork Research - They have groups in over a dozen cities and online
- Hello PingPong - Give your opinion regarding apps and websites
- Mindswarms - Give your opinion via video and earn up to $50.

A 529 plan is a college savings plan that allows you to save money by investing. The great thing about a 529 plan is your money grows, tax-free, as long as the funds are used for educational purposes. Other great features of 529 plans are 1) You can start saving for as low as $10 a paycheck, 2) Many plans offer payroll deduction, 3) There are tons of matching programs. Therefore, when you deposit so much, a company or your State may match your investment up to a particular dollar amount, and 4) Friends and Family can contribute to your 529 plan as birthday, baptismal, and bar mitzvah gifts, or for any other reason. They even have 529 gift cards! My nephew, 8-year-old sensation and collaborating author in this book Justyn, has won multiple contests and he has been awarded 1000s into his 529 college savings plan! Y'all college savings have never been so easy.

529 Plans

- Saving for College - Contests, opportunities, and information regarding 529 plans

- College Savings Plans Network - Contests, options, and details on 529 plans

- National Association of State Treasures - Lists 529 plans for all 50 States

- EVERFI - Scholarships and contests correlated with college savings

- UPromise - An easy-to-navigate 529 plan

In my number one best-selling workbook, **The Scholarship Doctor is In! 5 Easy Steps to a FREE Degree!** I discuss Ranking Up. In my opinion, one of the easiest ways to go to college for free is to graduate at the top of your class. Did you know there were scholarships for finishing as valedictorian, salutatorian, and in the top 5%, 10% even as much as the top 35% of your class? As valedictorian of my high school, I won five full-ride scholarships. Because of my high grades in college, I landed two full rides to graduate school. So, it is possible at any age to use class rank to go to college for FREE. Look at this list of scholarships available to you for going to school, earning good grades, and finishing at the top of your class. Congrats!

Class Rank

- Alcorn State University - Valedictorian and Salutatorian Scholarships
- Vincennes University - Valedictorian and Salutatorian Scholarships
- Malone Scholarship Program - Attend a Secondary School for Free
- PLEXUSS Foundation - Salutatorian Scholarship
- Oakwood University - Valedictorian Scholarship

Okay! You have five viable options that can and will help you attend college debt free, start a business using other people's money, or simply have as side hustles to your current income streams. I hope you will reach out to me and let me know which avenue you tried out or maybe you will be super bold and do all five! I would love to hear from you. Please follow me on Tik Tok and Instagram @scholarshipdr and let me know about your successes as you go to college for FREE!

You Can Go to College for FREE!

Lili St. Christopher

Founder and Chief Executive Officer of the College Bound Village (CBV) LLC

Mrs. Lili St. Christopher, better known as "Silver Lining Lili" is the founder and Chief Executive Officer of the College Bound Village (CBV) LLC. A native of East St. Louis, Illinois, Lili has over 25 years of experience in the financial services industry and her mission is to empower over 100,000 parents and scholars with scholarship and college resource information. The CBV motto of "Let's Get This Money for College" transcends several platforms including a 5,000-member private Facebook group that she started in 2019 when her son earned over $500,000 in college scholarships. Lili's intention is to bring together goal-oriented parents of college bound scholars to teach them proven scholarship strategies so that we can break generational curses, live abundantly, retire with ease, travel the world, and manifest God's glory as debt-free empty-nesters.

Lili earned a Bachelor's degree in Business Administration from Washington University in St. Louis, MO, and a MBA from Harding University in Searcy, AR.

collegeboundvillage.org | lili@collegeboundvillage.org
@collegeboundvillage - Facebook, LinkedIn, IG and YouTube

Veterans Benefits Matter

By: Lili St. Christopher

2023 is a year of milestones for my family.

I celebrated my 50th birthday on May 3rd.

My husband and I are on track to celebrate our 25th wedding anniversary on July 1st.

And my daughter, Laila, celebrated her 18th birthday and graduated from high school.

Watching her walk across the stage with a rainbow of colorful honor cords draped over her graduation gown gives me chills in a good way. Hearing the principal call her full government name, with Summa Cum Laude after it, makes me want to cry and scream all at the same time.

I'm crying happy tears of joy that she is achieving a milestone in life and our family is here to witness it.

I'm screaming "Hallelujah" to know that in a few short months, Laila will begin her freshman year at the University of California – San Diego. This is her dream school, and she plans to major in Pharmaceutical Science.

Laila applied to more than 20 colleges and was offered over $1 million in scholarships, including a full tuition scholarship to Fordham University in New York.

And she did it all during a global pandemic while working two part-time jobs and balancing several extracurricular activities and community service.

I wish I could tell you that I'm surprised by her academic achievements.

However, Laila has been an exceptional scholar since grade school demonstrating a high level of intellectual curiosity, learning agility, and focus.

I remember when she graduated from picture books to reading chapter books. She would always count the chapter numbers aloud as she expanded her vocabulary. And her big brother was right there encouraging her along the way.

She also saw him excel in high school and college.

Our son, Lorne II, is wrapping up his fifth and final year at the University of Missouri-St. Louis (UMSL) majoring in Mechanical Engineering. He accepted a full-ride Opportunity Scholarship from UMSL as well as a Type 7 full tuition scholarship from the Air Force ROTC. Lorne is currently interning at Boeing and will be joining the Air Force as an officer after graduation.

He was offered over $500,000 in scholarships in 2019 when he graduated from high school.

The benefit of Lorne going to college close to home, and moving back home temporarily during the pandemic, helped them establish a stronger relationship.

You might call it "trauma bonding" but I choose to call it "sibling bonding."

Lorne wasn't quite "California Dreaming" like Laila as his deciding factor for attending college was graduating with no debt.

And so far, he is stepping into his future debt free.

New Chapter, Same Book (The Trilogy)

Both of my children had a strong support system as they prepared for college.

You might say they had a village, both literally and figuratively, as they were surrounded by people who encouraged them to aspire to the 3 Ps: preparation, prayer, and a plan.

Let me explain.

After my son earned so many scholarships, I had several friends and family members asking me how he did it and if I could help them. To help make it easier for me, I started a private Facebook Group in 2019 called the College Bound Village (CBV).

This passion project turned into a thriving community of 5,000+ members and serves as a foundation for families to learn about college-bound success in a positive and encouraging environment.

I'm on a mission to empower 100,000 families with scholarships and college resources to increase financial literacy and build generational wealth.

I intend to bring together goal-oriented parents of college-bound scholars to teach them proven scholarship strategies so that we can break generational curses, live abundantly, retire with ease, travel the world, and manifest God's glory as debt-free empty-nesters.

The most impactful scholarship strategy for my daughter was directly related to my husband who didn't finish college.

He graduated from high school and immediately enlisted in the Navy, wasting no time towards a laser focus in pursuit of a military career.

Little did he realize that life was going to throw him a curve ball and in less than two years, his dream was cut short. With an Honorable Discharge and a 10 percent service-connected disability, he left the military walking using walking sticks.

He fought for over 10 years to increase his service-connected benefits and eventually, he was able to get to 100 percent disability before our children completed high school.

As a result, both qualified for Chapter 35 benefits which were instrumental in Laila getting an in-in-state tuition exemption which lowered her tuition by about $30,000 a year.

Lili also utilized Chapter 35 Benefits while earning her MBA debt-free in 2018.

Delayed, but not Denied – 4 Steps to Apply for a Rating Increase

If you're a veteran with a service-connected disability and have a spouse or child that desires to go to college, I highly suggest that you pursue getting 100 percent disability.

Dependents between the ages of 18 to 26 (8 years) can receive $1,400 per month for a maximum of 45 months for full-time students.

Here are four important steps to getting started to file for a VA disability rating increase:

1. Gather Medical Evidence:

    The first step is to collect all medical records from the VA as well as any other doctors outside of the VA system. This includes emergency room visits, hospitalization records, and any other documentation that supports your claim for an increased disability rating.

    It may be necessary to obtain statements from healthcare providers who can attest to the severity of your condition and its impact on your daily life. These statements should detail the specific limitations and symptoms you experience.

2. Connect with a Veterans Service Organization (VSO):

    Contact a Veterans Service Organization (VSO) such as the Disabled American Veterans (DAV) or Veterans of Foreign Wars (VFW) to advocate on your behalf. VSOs have trained representatives who can assist you in navigating the VA system and filing your claim. They can also provide free guidance on the best way to document information and the specific language to use that can make the difference between getting denied or approved for an increase in your rating.

3. File for an Increased Rating:

Once you have all the necessary paperwork, you should submit a formal request for an increased disability rating to the VA.

Provide a clear and detailed explanation of why you believe your condition warrants a higher rating. Reference specific medical evidence, symptoms, and limitations that support your claim.

This involves completing and submitting VA Form 21-526EZ, "Application for Disability Compensation and Related Compensation Benefits." This form can be submitted electronically, by mail, or hand delivered to a local VA office.

If you mail the paperwork, I suggest using tracking and/or getting a signature confirmation. If you hand deliver the paperwork, make sure to get a timestamp. Either way, don't forget to keep a copy of all the paperwork you submit.

4. Attend VA Compensation and Pension (C&P) Exams:

    The VA may schedule a Compensation and Pension (C&P) exam to evaluate the severity of your condition. These exams are typically conducted by VA doctors or contracted medical professionals.

    During the C&P exam, be prepared to discuss your medical history, symptoms, limitations, and how your condition affects your daily life. Be honest and thorough in providing relevant information during the examination. Stick to the facts and stay focused on the specific service-connected illnesses that are documented in your medical files.

In closing this chapter, I'd like to thank my husband for his service to our country and his dedication to our family. I also encourage all military personnel and veterans to be relentless in pursuing the benefits that they have earned. For the spouses of those veterans, be patient, be kind, and be encouraged.

Let's Get This Money for College!

You Can Go to College for FREE!

Marilyn Gilbert-Mitchell

Founder of MGM College Services LLC

Marilyn Gilbert-Mitchell, a 25-year educator, believes all students can pursue some form of education beyond high school as a ramp into their next part of life. As founder of MGM College Services LLC, she provides college planning services for 9th-12th grade students and families directly and through schools and organizations.

Since focusing on college planning, Marilyn Gilbert-Mitchell has directly assisted nearly 220+ students in securing 1,220+ college acceptances and over $17.5 million in confirmed scholarships. To date, she has visited over 200 college campuses and blends college knowledge, experiences, research, and resources to create materials that increase results. Helping students WIN with college and supporting families through these transitions are her life's missions.

Gilbert-Mitchell embeds skills and experiences acquired during 30+ years in corporate, college, cultural, community, and high school arenas. These include a high school teacher, college instructor, administrator, and Girl Scout Leader. Her background is strengthened by a bachelor's degree in English; three master's degrees; graduate certificate in College Admissions Counseling; and as an Illinois licensed educator. Additionally, Gilbert- Mitchell serves through her faith, as a 20+ year Girl Scout Leader, and proud member of Delta Sigma Theta Sorority, Inc.

"With proper planning, college is more than possible."

**mgmcollegeservices.com | info@mgmcollegeservices.com
Instagram & Twitter @mgmcollegesvcs**

Family Matters

By: Marilyn Gilbert-Mitchell

When discussing ways to pay for college, conversations focus on tuition, room, board, and books. Expenses often overlooked are transportation, toiletries, supplies, groceries, technology, and medications. Additionally, an underused resource for students' personal, career, mental, and financial support is family.

"One moment we brought our parents to class to share the scholarships we had received from schools. It helped me, help them, understand a glimpse of what we were working toward. My parents started supporting me, and that made it better for me to continue doing the work I needed to with their support and understanding."

Quote from a former student, now a college graduate and higher education representative

As the daughter, sister, niece, and friend of teachers, I knew the power of education and grew up with the academic expectation that college was required. That didn't bother me, as I didn't know anything different. Yet, it did not occur to me other students without similar examples or immediate family members were also college graduates.

When my children reached middle school grades, I told them they were going to college and needed scholarships to get there. As a parent, I meant to save money each month; I really did try. Then life kept life-ing, and money was used, reallocated, and replaced. I did not give my daughters deep details about our financial situation. After all, I was raised in a time when parents did not share their business with children or explain too much. But I explicitly, directly, and frequently told my daughters they would go to college on scholarships, and the family would help.

As a high school teacher, I saw and heard adults redirect or discount students' college dreams with comments that hurt my heart. "Not everyone is college material." "Have you considered cosmetology school, since your hair is always done so well?" "College is not for everyone. Let's find something else for you."

Hearing students recount these experiences and seeing their heads lower, eyes swell up, and voices soften set me on fire. I decided to fight for students and stand with them to reach their college goals. Doing this meant learning more about the college process and building a foundation for students to not only survive but thrive.

Many of my students wanted to go to college but did not know how. Some kept talking to the wrong people…. those who weren't supportive, shared negative experiences and had nothing good to say. I decided to be the bridge and created in-class and after-school activities to expose students to college and career experiences, excursions, and examples. One activity was "Bring Your Parent to Class Week," a time each semester for students' parents to attend one class, sit in the back of the room, and be a silent observer. This allowed parents to see what we were working on in class, earn extra credit for students, connect with me for "tag team" support, and support the learning process. I must add there were moments of comedy, light embarrassment, and angelic behavior with parents in the room.

"You mean my mom would stay in the class all period?"

"What if they both want to come?"

"You don't really want to talk to them, do you?"

After each class, parents shared their thoughts. Students "felt the love" and were proud their parents came. For students with challenging family situations, I gave the option to bring a "parent alternate" if the parent/guardian sent a note confirming the representative's approved participation.

Let's talk about how parents, guardians, and trusted adults can support students' college goals. Before we get there, it is important to mention that college is more than a 4-year institution. It comes in many forms from vocational, trade, and technical schools to certification programs, community colleges (2 years), and colleges and universities (4 years).

For this chapter, I use an expanded definition to include all education beyond high school. This is critically important with the increase in technology-based careers and the need for more advanced training and professional skills, even in careers that do not require college degrees.

What's the first step?

1 Check your connections and create strong networks. There are various networks needed for college and career success. People often think about their friends in social arenas, yet they also offer hidden connections. What do I mean?

We all have friends, family, neighbors, church members, colleagues, and others around us. Each person connects to others and can be a link to opportunities, open doors, and introductions.

These various networks provide professional, personal, and private support. Let's take them one at a time.

Professional support includes job shadowing, college and career conversations, building strong skills and habits, and discussing colleges that excel in specific career fields.

If you're an adult, parent, mentor, or coach, do you have friends and colleagues in different career fields? Are some of these careers of interest to your teens or their friends?

If you're a student, what are the careers of your friends' parents and family members? How often do you spend time with them or at their houses? How can you have college and career conversations with them about the path to their current professions?

Personal Support means having understanding and empathetic connections with others, finding trusted people to bounce ideas and share goals with steps, and increasing success through accountability. Especially during the late teen to young adult years, students may not talk as much to their parents and still need positive, personal support. This time of transition merges learning more about self, building successful habits and behaviors, and maturing into adulthood.

Private support is your confidential, inner circle of people to discuss challenges and mistakes, operate in a no-judgment zone, and celebrate successes. This #SupportSquad may be a handful of people to discuss thoughts, fears, feelings, and visions in a safe environment. Such support is critical to positive, trusting, supportive, and healthy relationships with yourself and others.

2 The second step is **to strengthen social-emotional learning and emotional intelligence**.

"*Did I do that?*" Whenever Steve Urkel said this iconic phrase on the television show, *Family Matters*, it made light of some silly, messy, or chaotic situation. While funny on tv then, this does not transfer well to real life now.

When students do not develop these skills, they can turn into adults who struggle with interpersonal, intrapersonal, and relational skills. How can we work in the community to support student's growth and development into responsible, respectful, and productive global citizens?

What are some of these skills to start in younger grades that lead to positive, productive, and successful adults?

According to CASEL (Collaborative for Academic, Social, and Emotional Learning), a leader in social-emotional learning (SEL), the five competencies are self-awareness, self-management, social awareness, relationship skills, and responsible decision-making. Research reports, "**86%** [of parents and caregivers] say social and emotional learning has become even more important since the pandemic." *McGraw Hill, 2021*

How do these skills connect to college and career success? They link to continuing healthy, strong relationships; self-managing emotions and actions; developing problem-solving and decision-making skills; creating hands of action and hearts of service; and building habits for success in all areas of life.

Imagine how different the world would be with more people - children, youth, young adults, adults, seniors - living these skills daily.

3 The third step is **to stand on the foundations of family and faith.**

What if students do not have supportive families, faith in themselves, or faith in God? That happens for a variety of reasons, and I have seen examples in over two decades as an educator. I believe family is more than those you are blood-related to and also includes the village you choose.

Families are "home plate" and the foundation of our lives that connect to mind, body, and spiritual wellness. They represent safety, protection, love, and support with people you are not afraid to be yourself with and openly share your highlights, hiccups, and hurdles.

Family support allows for growth, maturity, and identity as well as a safe place to live authentically. Along with faith that grounds and guides, family weave threads between past, present, and purpose.

While in college, how can students' family networks help them?

- Care packages
- Encouraging notes, cards, and texts
- Gift cards, money orders, or cash
- Surprise visits
- "Just because" gifts
- Grocery and food deliveries
- Home cooked meals
- Bible study, prayer calls, and online family worship
- Mental, emotional, and physical wellness check-ins

Different networks serve different purposes and timeframes. Some are situational or seasonal, temporary or permanent, and surface or intense.

Who are in your professional, personal, and private networks? How can they help you, <u>and</u> how can you help them?

Take a moment and create a list of twenty (20) people across these three (3) categories. Reach out to them individually, spend time together, and genuinely connect. Don't ask for anything at first; take time to get to know each other. If you're a student, talk to your parents and share your list and plans.

"No man is an island. No one stands alone." This writing in John Donne's 17th-century poem stands true today. Choose your support systems wisely and know connections can propel students forward into greatness or push them backwards into mediocrity. Family matters!

Shymika Stephenson-Davison

Owner & Lead Consultant of PreCollege Solutions

Shymika Stephenson-Davison is native of Vivian, Louisiana and resides in Dallas, Texas. She is Owner & Lead Consultant of PreCollege Solutions, a College Readiness Consulting & Coaching Company. She completed her bachelor's and master's degrees in business administration and has a certificate in Non-Profit Management.

Her expertise in the college admission process, scholarship process, financial aid process, and youth development spans nearly twelve years. She is often a guest contributor and blogger for various outlets such as Yahoo and Real Simple in the areas of college and scholarship prep.

precollegesolutions.com | info@precollegesolutions.com

Instagram @PreCollegeSolutions

College Prep Exams can save you MONEY!

By: Shymika Stephenson-Davison

"You're my first client to ever become a National Merit Finalist". I yelled to Samson over the phone. I don't know if he ever realized how huge and rare this honor was. The top 1%, or about 16,000 students across the country, are named National Merit Semifinalists. This is an honor in itself, and it also means you could go on to be named a Finalist and receive scholarship money. This happened to Samson in his junior year of high school by taking the PSAT (Preliminary Scholastic Aptitude Test). I consider the PSAT a hidden jewel for potential scholarships similar to the SAT, ACT, AP, and CLEP exams. There are two reasons why families do not capitalize on these tests regarding paying for college. The first reason is the lack of information. If families are not investing in college prep outside of their child's high school, then it will be evident by not understanding the importance of these exams. A high school student who produces a high score on SAT, ACT, and PSAT will be placed in an elite marketing group fostered by College board and colleges will begin offering scholarships as early as sophomore and junior year. Did you know that? Most parents and guardians do not. The second reason is time. For most high school students and families, they believe that the college admission process starts their senior year. Most of these exams are useless by senior year which means the opportunities have expired.

Below is a chart of college readiness exams that can help alleviate paying for college.

You Can Go to College for FREE!

Exam	Definition	Best Time to Start Prep	Acceptable Scores	Outcomes
PSAT	Stands for Preliminary SAT, which is used to prepare high school sophomores and juniors who intend to take the SAT for admission during their senior year.	Summer prior to sophomore year	Top 75% ranking	Extremely high scores can lead to National Merit Semi-Finalist & Finalist. This is a top academic honor, which leads to scholarships.
SAT & ACT	A standardized college entrance test administered by the College Board & ACT.	Sophomore year	Your state of residence SAT & ACT average. (Can be located on CollegeBoard website.)	College acceptance and scholarship awards can depend on the score. Listed under credit-by-exam, the ACT and SAT can perform double duty: college admissions and college credit. Earn an acceptable score according to college guidelines and gain English and math credits. Moreover, credits may or may not count toward GPA.
AP	A high school course that teaches material ordinarily for college students.	Freshman year	A score of 3 or higher is considered passing.	Receiving college credit if you pass the course and exam
IB	IB exams are recognized for college credit in a way similar to AP exams. You don't have to earn the IB Diploma to get credit for individual classes, Colleges give credit course by course.	Freshman year (Depends on the high school)	A score in the 40s will make you a more competitive candidate academically (note: non-academic factors are at play), but a 38+ is considered a good IB score.	IB Diploma and Courses are favorable among Ivy league universities. You can also receive college credit.
CLEP	The College-Level Examination Program (CLEP) are tests you can take for college credit for your undergraduate degree, rather than completing lengthier courses.	Any grade level	The American Council on Education (ACE) recommends colleges grant credit for scores 50 or higher, but individual institutions can set their policies.	Receive college credit, if you pass the exam.

Samson became my client in the second semester of his sophomore year. As a ninth grader, he didn't realize high school would be extremely challenging. Making the initial mistake of not taking his academics seriously during his freshman year hurt his GPA. The rigorous academic classes took a toll on his self-confidence. During the summer before his junior year, I introduced him to PSAT, its purpose, and its importance. I told him that if he did well on the PSAT, he may become a National Merit Semi-Finalist. Colleges would recruit him for academics. In disbelief, he still decided to work throughout the summer on practice tests and timed drills. In October, he was ready. After the test, he said, "I think I failed." I encouraged him as we waited for months for the notification. At the end of his junior year, he received notification, he was a National Merit Semi-Finalist. We were excited about this honor. He could add this academic honor to his college applications. Then in his senior year, he received the National Merit Finalist status. In this status, you can receive scholarships in three categories:

1. National Merit Scholarships

    You receive a one-time scholarship of $2,500.

2. Corporate-Sponsored Merit Scholarships and Special Scholarships

    The second type of scholarship offered by the NMSC is a corporate-sponsored scholarship. Two types of corporate-sponsored scholarships are available to students who enter the NMSC: corporate-sponsored merit scholarships, and corporate-sponsored special scholarships.

As is the case with National Merit Scholarships, Finalists are given automatic consideration for corporate-sponsored scholarships based on their applications and the information they provide about parental employment, intended majors, and career plans.

3. College-Sponsored Merit Scholarships Finalists who receive neither a National Merit Scholarship nor a corporate-sponsored scholarship are considered for college-sponsored scholarships. These do not include Ivy League universities. There is also an application process. Fortunately, Samson was able to receive a $2,500 National Merit Scholarship and $10,000 from Liberty Mutual Scholarship Foundation for excelling on a test. In addition to his scholarships, he received college credit through his AP courses administered through his high school. Many people already are familiar with advanced placement courses and their benefits. Let's review. High school students have the option as early as freshman year to start taking advanced placement courses. AP courses are free high school courses that teach material ordinarily intended for college students in subjects such as English, Physics, Computer Science, University History, etc.

After completion of the advanced placement course, a standardized test is taken, for which they may receive college credit if they pass. For example, if a high school student took two AP courses and passed the exams each year until they graduated high school. The high school student could start college nearly a sophomore, alleviating the cost of their freshman year of college. This has prompted me to spread this information to high school students and parents about the importance of understanding college entrance exams. Here are three tips for maximizing scholarships through these college entrance exams.

1. Conduct your research on which exam(s) is best for your teen.
2. Communicate with your teen's counselor about these exams and ask for resources.
3. Seek test preparation/tutoring services to enhance your teen's knowledge.

You Can Go to College for FREE!

Carol Ben-Davies
Founder and CEO of College Bound Determination

Carol Ben-Davies is the founder and CEO of College Bound Determination, a guiding force for parents in strengthening their children for the realities of college. With over 20 years of experience serving at top universities in the US, Carol Ben-Davies has made meaningful contributions in the areas of Undergraduate Admissions, Fraternity and Sorority Life, Student Leadership Development, Student Advocacy and Support, and Diversity, Equity, and Inclusion. Throughout her career, Carol has assisted countless college students and their parents, helping them navigate the challenges of college life, from breakthroughs to breakdowns.

During her tenure as Assistant Dean of Students, Carol served on the front lines, supporting students who faced academic, social, emotional, financial, and mental struggles. She also guided parents in addressing the damaging mental health challenges, threatening experiences, and intense social pressures that led to their child's mental and academic breakdown. Witnessing the suffering of these young individuals motivated Carol to create College Bound Determination to prevent such breakdowns.

Carol is dedicated to assisting parents and organizations who are determined to protect students and their success beyond high school. Carol proactively prepares students with a solid foundation to increase their emotional intelligence, mindsets, and skillsets. By equipping them with necessary tools, Carol helps students repel the common college pitfalls that can transform their "college dream" into a nightmare. Through her mental health advocacy, she replaces mental health breakdowns with breakthroughs in college success.

Carol holds a M.Ed. in Higher Education Administration from Loyola University Chicago and a B.A. from the University of North Carolina at Chapel Hill. She is a Certified Gallup-Certified Strengths Coach, a certified QPR Suicide Prevention Instructor and a Strong's Interest Inventory Certified Practitioner.

carolbendavies.com
@carol ben-davies on all social media platforms

The Hidden Costs of Losing a Full Scholarship

By: Carol Ben-Davies

"Success in college is not just about getting in, but also about navigating the hidden costs and challenges along the way."

~Carol Ben-Davies~

After years of working hard throughout high school to secure a college scholarship, Elizabeth made her dream a reality by getting a full-merit scholarship to her dream college. She was proud of herself, and her family, who otherwise would not have been able to afford to send her to college, shared in her pride. She became the pride of her community, and there were so many expectations that Elizabeth would thrive in college and beyond.

Unfortunately, as the first semester unfolded, Elizabeth faced unforeseen challenges that threatened the goals that she and everyone rooting for her had for her college journey. Despite her strong academic record, which included taking Advanced Placement classes and maintaining over a 4.0 GPA throughout high school, the rigorous demands of college work became overwhelming. She felt lost, unprepared, and ashamed she couldn't grasp things as easily as she had. She began to withdraw from everything and everyone she knew. Unsure who to trust and turn to, her anxiety and self-doubt grew. The burden of maintaining her scholarship and the fear of disappointing her parents mounted. Like many students who enter college with great promise, the academic pressure affected even the most promising students. No student expects to experience academic setbacks.

The harsh reality is that there are many college students like Elizabeth who expected their full scholarship would be secure, often overlooking the importance of preparing for college beyond admissions and scholarships so they are more equipped for the common college pitfalls that may arise.

Preparing for college can be a stressful time for families. As parents, we always want what's best for our children. When it comes to the cost of college, tuition and fees, room and board, books, and other expenses, how to pay for it all are often the primary concerns for families. Is that why you picked up this book? To learn how to attend college for free. However, it is crucial to consider the potential consequences if a student were to lose a full scholarship for any reason. There are hidden costs that extend beyond obtaining a scholarship. In this chapter, we will explore these hidden costs and provide strategies to help avoid common college pitfalls that impact students even if they receive thousands of dollars in scholarships. By being more strategic and planning ahead, we can alleviate stress, save valuable time, and money and create the generational legacy we desire for our children.

Despite concerns about college affordability, crippling student loan debt, and questions about the relevancy of a college degree amid a post-COVID economy, attending college remains a top priority for many families. Education continues to be, as Horace Mann said 175 years ago, " the great equalizer of the conditions of men—the balance wheel of the social machinery." And the more education one has, the greater the likelihood of reaping the benefits financially, emotionally and socially, and economically. College, including two-year community colleges and trade schools, matters.

By shifting our focus beyond just how to get into and how to pay for college, we help emphasize successfully planning for the entire college journey. From college admissions, the transition from high school to college to the smooth and bumpy ride toward college graduation, the ultimate goal.

A full scholarship often comes with academic and financial expectations that the scholarship will be maintained all four years with the same level of excellence it took to obtain the scholarship but in my professional experience, that is not always the case. Losing this scholarship can disrupt a student's educational trajectory, affecting their motivation, focus, and mental health.

Here are just a few of the hidden costs you must prepare your child to avoid:

The Cost of Failing to Maintain Academic Standards

One hidden cost that can affect a student's college journey and their ability to maintain their scholarship is poor grades as a result of ineffective study habits and poor time management. Especially when a student like Elizabeth has made all A's since Kindergarten, it is unfathomable to scholars and their families that they will earn grades below an A but that can be a sad reality, one I helped students and parents navigate as a college administrator and now as a college success coach and strategist. Many scholars were able to coast through high school with minimal effort earning As and accolades without having to study. Poor studying and poor time management skills as a result of newfound freedom can lead to subpar grades and a waste of valuable semesters.

By instilling effective study habits, time management skills, and productivity techniques, parents can help their children achieve academic success. Investing time in developing these skills early on will make a significant difference in their college experience. We should also help students understand they are more than their grades so that when they fail academically, they don't feel like failures in life. It's a fundamental mindset shift needed to bounce back from academic setbacks.

The Hidden Cost of Selecting the Wrong Major

Many students enter college without a clear idea of what they want to study and why. Elizabeth always knew she wanted to be a doctor. But as she failed her Organic Chemistry class, she began to question why she said she wanted to be a doctor in the first place. It is entirely normal for them to be unsure. The pressure to figure out what you want to do for, what many students believe is, the rest of their lives, can be heavy. Many students, even very focused and high achieving students who knew since they were 8 years old what their career would be, may change their mind. Statistically, about 80% of students change their major at least once while in college, and 75% change it three or four times. This lack of clarity can result in wasted time and additional expenses, expenses a scholarship may or may not cover. This can result in taking extra classes or delaying graduation. The average college student does not graduate in four years. According to the National Center for Education Statistics (NCES), the average student takes around 6 years to complete their undergraduate degree. If renewable, most scholarships are designed to only cover four years. Changing your major in college often results in taking extra courses, meeting different requirements and prerequisites, and taking more time to complete the degree.

To address this, parents can help their children gain more clarity about their academic and career interests. Encourage them to explore various assessments that increase a student's self-awareness. These tools can provide valuable insights and guide students towards a well-suited major that allows them to hit the ground running into opportunities that set up their career success.

The Hidden Cost of an Unaddressed Mental Health Illness in College

While the focus on college often revolves around academics, financials, and career opportunities, it is vitally important to recognize the profound impact of mental health on the overall well-being and academic performance of college students. There has long been a mental health crisis on college campuses. For over 20 years college mental health centers have not been able to keep up with the demand for their services. COVID heightened the concern and attention to student mental health. One of the significant hidden costs is the detrimental effect on academic performance. Students' grades suffer due to mental health challenges. The pressure of maintaining grades, dealing with the level of academic rigor they were not used to in high school, and keeping their scholarship can place a significant burden on students. Students may not have the techniques and coping strategies to navigate challenges. It is not uncommon for students to isolate themselves from their family and friends and stop attending classes. But not only do they withdraw from people due to failing grades they may end up withdrawing from all their classes and losing tuition and fees as a result.

Unfortunately, it takes a mental health crisis to learn the life skills taught in therapy. Families can be proactive by focusing as much on students' mental well-being as they do on their academic excellence. Mental health is health as the slogan says. Promote the message that there is strength in asking for and seeking help. Begin self-care practices early and as a family. Incorporate stress management techniques such as deep breathing, setting boundaries, and healthy eating and exercise habits.

Navigating the college journey can be challenging for both parents and students. By understanding the hidden costs beyond tuition and fees, parents can take a proactive approach to supporting their children. Encourage clarity in choosing a major, foster effective study habits and time management skills, take full advantage of campus resources and staff, and prioritize mental health. Remember, your child's happiness, health, and overall well-being are essential.

Nathan McCalla

Teen Life & Performance Coach

Nathan McCalla is a Teen and Young Adult Life Coach, Mental Performance Coach, National Keynote Speaker and Educator

Since studying under some of the most prolific leaders in the world on mindset, behavior change, and goal achievement, Nathan has spent years pouring into the lives of teens and young adults, getting them unstuck in life by helping them realize their natural gifts, reach their dreams, and see the endless possibilities for their lives.

From the ups and downs of college - failing multiple classes (even failing the same class twice!), facing peer pressure of friends he admired most, changing majors twice, and the experience of playing college football cut short, to discovering his natural gift and true passion in school and finding the people he truly belonged to - Nathan shares with you his story from the mistakes he made in college so you don't have to.

Want to make sure you keep going to college for free once you get there? Join Nathan as he shows you exactly how.

Facebook https://www.facebook.com/nathan.mccalla.7
Messenger at http://m.me/nathan_mccalla.

Four Keys to Keep You Going to College For Free Once You Get There

By: Nathan McCalla

There are clear actions in life that if we do them, we nearly guarantee successful outcomes for ourselves. The cause and effects of these actions are called "principles" which act as rules for living.

I'll give you an example. When I graduated college and began working full-time as a teacher, I didn't see a dentist for three years because it simply never felt important enough to do. And besides, I was an adult - I knew how to brush my teeth.

Well, when I finally went to the dentist, I was utterly shocked by the news I received: I had not one, not two, but THREE cavities. But where had I gone wrong all this time? Well, it turns out I had been brushing my teeth consistently. But, I had not been *flossing.* This was a costly mistake! I had to pay almost $1,000 to get my cavities filled. All because I didn't floss??? Yep, not flossing slowly led to my teeth getting into bad shape. Now, do you think I floss these days? You bet I do. I take it seriously because that small action cost me a lot. As flossing is just one example, you can probably guess that there are a ton of principles out there that will help you in life. And here specifically we'll look at the four most important principles that will keep you going to college for free once you get there (we'll call them our "Four Keys" to remember them more easily).

But before I share the four keys, I have a secret for you. You may expect that what I'm about to share with you comes from years of doing the right things and having a lot of success throughout my college career. While I eventually *would* find my way, my college career was anything but successful. It's actually because I did *NOT* do a lot of the right things, but rather, made so many mistakes that I can now show you exactly what works and what is truly most important to focus on to be successful in college.

Just like with Michael Jordan's famous quote, he says it's because of all the many times he has failed over his career that are the very REASON why he succeeds.

And that's part of the secret; being successful is not a direct result of having success. Being successful is a result that comes from trying, failing, learning, and trying again. And as we keep doing this over time, we grow and become successful. Besides, most people learn better from failure and mistakes (either theirs or someone else's) than they do from success. This is why I share my mistakes and failures with you here in this chapter, so you can learn and apply these principles to be successful, both in college and in life.

Now that I've shared the secret with you, are you ready to learn the four keys to keep you going to college for free once you get there? If so, let's begin!

Key #1: Choose the Right People

I honestly didn't want to, but it was my freshman year of college when I tried illegal substances for the first time in my life. I was with a group of teammates I enjoyed hanging out with and unconsciously I appreciated the acceptance I got from them. It wasn't until later on that I realized how pointless that activity was though and how I took for granted the football scholarship I could have lost because of this (34,000 a year at that time for anyone on a full-ride scholarship). Not to mention, taking for granted all the sacrifices and hard work my mom put in to get me to college.

Choosing the right people is so important because who we spend time with is exactly who we become like. Call it your circle of influence, your environment, your top five - whatever you like. As the quote goes, "Show me your friends, and I'll show you your future." Who we spend time with is the number one determining factor for where we go in life. Think about the language you speak, the accent you have, the foods you like, and even the movie references you know. These are all impacted by *who* you've been around over time. And believe it or not, we are still influenced by other people as we become adults. This is why it's SO important to choose the right people to spend our time around as it will directly impact where you go.

Key #2: Find Your Mentor

This is something I feel like I got right in college. As a low-income and first-generation student, I got the chance to be a part of TRIO, a student support services organization. This is where I met my mentor Ron, my TRIO advisor. Ron was in his early 30's and oozed confidence and charisma, yet he had experienced a lot of hard times for his age. Ron would end up being there for me during my senior year of college when it felt like life was falling apart. This is when having him as my mentor through Trio would mean everything to me. Finding a mentor is vital because it's having someone who has been in your shoes and knows what it's like to be where you are. They can look at your situation with deep understanding, and they can give you an objective, outside perspective because they don't have all the feelings attached to whatever is going on in your world.

Key #3: Raise Your Game - What got you here is not what will keep you here.

I was a pretty good football player in high school, even earning the opportunity to play in multiple All-Star games after my senior year. But the truth is when I got to college, I never played in an official regular season game. Why? Because I did the same things that made me good in high school. But what I needed to do to be good in college was different - it was *next level*. Note that what gets you to college, won't be the same as what gets you through to graduating. You will need to raise the level of your game, just like my roommate Stan did. Stan told me that during high school, he was *very* average as a student, noting that his 2.8 GPA was the middle of his class. But when he got to college, he committed to raising his academic game and finished his college career with a 3.7 GPA as a Biology Pre-Med major.

Key #4: Solve x + y

No book about going to college would be complete without a little math, am I right? Jokes aside, this is not what you think. Do you know the term "x marks the spot" when referring to pirate treasure maps? X is the destination where the treasure is, and so it's the same principle. We must mark our destination, the place we're going. That means we create a vision for where our life is going, like setting a destination in your GPS. Setting the destination helps us determine the route to get there, aka the steps we need to get there.

What about y? Well, y isn't referring to the letter, but rather the word "why." Knowing "why" is knowing your reason for even going toward your destination in the first place. A phrase I love is, "If your why doesn't make you cry then it's just a lie" so make sure you take time to think and search in your heart what your why is because your why becomes the fuel and motivation to keep going, especially in difficult times. If there's something I know, it's that challenges will present themselves to you. So if you ever feel lost or lack motivation, find a quiet space or speak with someone you trust, and review your destination and you're why.

My friend, it took me years of failure and mistakes in college to learn these lessons and just how important the previous principles are to success. Just make sure to choose well the people you spend time with, find a wise mentor, take your actions to the next level, and solve for $x + y$. If you can do this, I assure you that you too, can keep going to college for free once you get there.

Nikayla Williams

Mechanical Engineer | Blogger

Nikayla Williams is a well-rounded, exceptionally accomplished young lady. Born in the Las Vegas valley, she always had high expectations and goals set for herself. She graduated high school in 2016 with an Advanced Honors Diploma and a multitude of community service experiences that allowed her to get accepted into acclaimed schools like Spelman College, Bethune Cookman University, and Florida Agricultural and Mechanical University (FAMU). She chose her beloved alma mater, Virginia State University, after deciding she wanted to have a more intimate college experience. This benefited her as she made new friends and colleagues at her university, even joining the National Society of Black Engineers, Sigma Alpha Pi (the National Society of Leadership and Success) and becoming a member of Delta Sigma Theta Sorority, Inc. Nikayla graduated college at her illustrious institution as Cum Laude with a Mechanical Engineering Technology B.S degree in May 2020.

nikaylawilliamz.com
@nikaylawilliamz on all social media platforms

Application Salvation:

The First Stepping Stone to Your College Career

By: Nikayla Williams

There I was, a freshman in high school. Finally entering into the big leagues. While most students were worried about what sports they would play, which classes would be the hardest, or who would be their date to homecoming, I had bigger fish to fry. How would I get into college? My mom and I read an article about a single mother whose four kids graduated college without any student loan debt. "We need to be doing what she's doing!" my mom admirably exclaimed. Through research, word of mouth, and a sheer stroke of luck, we were introduced to Rhea Watson, The Scholarship Doctor.

***

Meeting Rhea was a breath of fresh air. She was the silver lining. She sealed up the bottomless pit that formed in my stomach whenever I thought of college. During The Scholarship Solution's consultation class, Rhea inspired and encouraged attendees. My mother and I jotted down notes, not wanting to miss a drop of information. Rhea explained all the ways to attend college for free. Scholarships, grants, waivers! Oh my! What once seemed like a dream far off in the distance became a close tangible goal. The impossible now seemed possible. I was in the hands of a powerful and accomplished woman (and so are you since you are reading this book.). I trusted Rhea and knew if I did what she said, staying the course of high academics and extraordinary community service, I would go to college for free like the four siblings I read about.

***

My journey to going to college for free started by going to Rhea's office every Sunday. Although this was not an ideal high schooler's weekend, I nonetheless rolled up my sleeves and worked the plan; and with time, the funds began rolling in. I applied and applied, and applied some more. Although I had years to go before actually enrolling into an institution, I was able to secure funds from public and private organizations for my academics, my service to the community, and my personal skills, like poetry.

***

I finally knew how I was going to pay for college, but another question began to creep in: where was I going to attend? I began diving into search engines to look at different colleges. I heard about HBCUs so I started my research with one I was familiar with, Spelman College. When I scrolled through their website I saw beautiful, Black, educated women. I saw the campus they walked through, the classes they sat in, and the happiness they possessed. "I want to be one of those women," I said to myself.

***

I landed on their admissions page. I typed in all of my personal information, but as I continued scrolling, it asked me for payment information. Wait… It costs to apply to college?! (Y'all have to remember I'm a first generation college student, so this information was unknown to me.) I knew it would cost to attend school, and that basis was already being covered. Finding out I had to pay just to apply to colleges reopened the bottomless pit in my stomach. Do all schools cost or just this one? If they do cost, how much can the application be? What if I don't get in!? Will they reimburse me the money and then I can use it to apply somewhere else? There was a tightness forming around my chest. I was too young for a heart attack, but the thought of money going down the drain could make anyone faint. Thank God the Scholarship Doctor was in the house.

***

That next Sunday when I was sitting in Rhea's office, I asked my unnerving question. "Rheaaa..." I said in an unenthused voice.

"Yessss?" she responded knowing something was wrong.

"Does it cost to apply to school?"

"Well of course it does!" she belted out with a laugh. It was as though I had asked her if the sky was blue and money was green. The silver lining was shining and I could feel the pit in my stomach disappearing. I knew that her delighted response was not mockery of me, but confirmation that this was something that she was aware of and had already planned on helping me overcome when the time came. I am honored to share with you the information and guidance that was shared with me:

- Use awarded scholarship money for application fees;
- Ask your high school counselor for a waiver;
- Ask the college that you're applying to for a waiver;
- Demonstrate financial need and enroll into a free lunch program to receive their college waiver;
- Submit applications at local colleges fairs where fees are waived;
- Score high enough on the ACT or SAT;

- Get a Common App waiver and apply to multiple schools in the portal;

- Get a coalition waiver or an NACAC waiver;

- Or apply to colleges that don't require an application fee.

***

Although I didn't take every course of action listed above, receiving waivers from my counselor, applying to multiple schools with a one time fee through the Common App, and attending college fairs were all a tremendous time, money, and life saver. I'll never forget walking into my community center's college fair as a frightened soon to be college freshman. I stopped at nearly every table and filled out an application. I was there from dawn until dusk; another one of my high school weekend's gone. But! I got accepted into a handful of schools on the spot and even received some scholarships. In fact, applying at a college fair is actually how I got accepted into my alma mater, Virginia State University. And between you and me, they only offered me a $5,000 scholarship upon my initial acceptance. However, I kept my grades up and kept an open line of communication with the admissions office and they eventually offered me a full ride!

***

So students, parents or guardians, if you have stuck with me this far, I want you to know that it is more than possible to not only have your college tuition paid for, but the upfront cost of applying to college can be covered as well. It is imperative that you know, trust, and believe this. College can be one of those determining factors that alters the course of one's entire life. The application fee is a hurdle that unfortunately deters many folks from applying in the first place. You must try, and try again, and again. I will not pretend to say the journey is easy. I will not lie and say the journey is quick. It is indeed a studious and tedious one. However, Zig Ziglar once said, "there are no traffic jams along the extra mile," and he is right. Every year millions of dollars in scholarships are left on the table, unclaimed, because students won't try to reach for them. Sadly, they give up before they even begin. Please, do not be one of these students.

***

Would I give up my weekends to apply for scholarships and attend college fairs again? Absolutely, because like most challenging journeys, the reward in the end is worth it. Your college career— your future— is worth the effort.

You Can Go to College for FREE!

Zena Robinson-Wouadjou and Vanessa Emile
Co-founders | SchoolWideRead

Zena Robinson-Wouadjou (MSEd) and Vanessa Emile (MSEd, PhD Candidate) are the cofounders of SchoolWideRead (SWR Community, LLC). Zena is a mother, community activist and educator with 20 plus years of experience in curriculum, instruction and program design & facilitation. Her areas of expertise include literacy development, TESOL, ELA, Advanced Placement, CRSE, Restorative Practice, and College & Career Access and Success. She is passionate about creating spaces that affirm community, genius, liberation, and love.

Vanessa Emile is a dynamic educator with 10 years of experience in successfully moving students at different skill levels and from diverse backgrounds to achieve college readiness. She believes in meeting students where they are while offering them the tools and motivation to meet their academic goals and navigate the world in which they live.

SchoolWideRead

SchoolWideRead (SWR Community, LLC), is a literacy-focused program that creates culturally responsive, healing-centered frameworks for building literacy, community, scholarship, and social justice. SchoolWideRead partners with forward-thinking educators, school/ organization leaders, student groups, and family collectives across the country who share their vision of redefining what it means to teach, learn, and be in community.

schoolwideread.org | community@schoolwideread.org
Instagram @swrcommunity

Supporting The Dream:

From Community to Campus With Love

By: Zena Robinson-Wouadjou and Vanessa Emile | SchoolWideRead

Starting Something: The Story of SchoolWideRead Writing Challenge Scholarship

Looking back at our inaugural writing challenge competition back in February of 2013, we can still remember the excitement that had been building around the community discussion day and the school-wide celebration that preceded the announcement of our first scholarship winner.

As everyone proceeded from the third floor discussion space to the school's basement cafeteria, it was beautiful to witness the presence of the entire school body gathered in one space. Students, school administrators, parents, teachers, custodial engineers, parent coordinators, school secretaries, and community members— some seated, some standing— all waiting to hear who had won the competition.

While we were setting up the microphones and sound system, we noticed our 1st prize winner moving slowly towards a side door, preparing to take an "early leave" for the day. We made our way over to him before he could exit the building and asked him to "please stay." He responded positively with a reluctant smile, and took a seat in the audience.

At that point, he had no idea that his essay had been selected. In fact, no one in the school even knew what the winner would receive. After reading out the names of the 3rd and 2nd place winners (in a very dramatic Grammy Award style), we pulled out the final certificate. As we read his name, applause and shouts of "Yeah, Tye!" rose from the crowd. We invited the student to the front of the room and handed him a certificate and a small envelope (both purchased on our teacher salary budget from the local Staples). Gently opening the envelope, his eyes widened with surprise! He revealed its contents — a crisp $100 bill— to the audience and the SchoolWideRead Writing Challenge Scholarship was born.

Growing It: Transforming a Moment into a Mission

After awarding that first scholarship, there was one thing that became clear. Beyond the euphoria of the moment, we knew we wanted to continue supporting young people in pursuing college and helping them realize the highest visions of themselves.

Working primarily in communities and with student populations who have historically been excluded from the higher education process, it has always been important for us to ensure that our students and families know that although "college was not designed for everyone" to participate, today college can be a pathway for any student who chooses it. As we worked to make sure that all students, particularly those who have been underserved (students of color, divergent learners/ differently abled students, English language learners, students from immigrant families, and students from lower income households), have the tools and resources they need to access educational opportunities leading up to and through college, it became important for us to identify and remove, the greatest barriers to our young people's success, finances.

What We Learned

Consistently not having what you need can limit your ability to dream of what you desire. For many of our young people, their current financial situation makes a college education feel completely out of reach. As a result, some begin to edit the possibility of college out of the script of their imaginations— deciding to just stop wanting what appears to be impossible to have.

When you dilute the "flavor," you weaken the "juice". In many school environments, students are discouraged from being their "full selves." Over time, young people lose touch with their unique identity and voice— the very things that make them stand out and shine on college admissions and scholarship applications.

The "how" is just as important as the "what." Quite often, talented students miss the opportunity for earning scholarships simply because they lack experience and practice with the process of finding and applying for awards.

In examining each of these barriers, we have been able to design a solution-focused scholarship program that directly addresses the financial gaps preventing students from realizing the dream of college, creates scholarship campaigns that invite students to explore and bring their identity to the table, and offers a consistent structure and process for scholarship applications.

Building Together: A Culturally Responsive, Community Supported Scholarship Model

A major key to our success lies in our decision to work collectively with all of the stakeholders in the school and larger community. When we think about what made that first scholarship award assembly special, it was the inclusion of community. Being recognized and cheered on by one's school, family and neighborhood offers a sense of support and encouragement, which are instrumental in helping a student persist through college. That show of love and commitment should not begin and end with an awards ceremony.

The culturally responsive, community supported scholarship model invites the community to fully participate in the college going culture and process, including the financial support of the student. But what does that look like?

First, create regularly scheduled public-facing events (example: town halls, community problem-solving meetings) that bring the community together in support of learning and idea sharing. How does this help? Students get to practice adding their voice to the conversation and listening to the perspectives of their teachers, friends, parents, and mentors— skills which they will be expected to demonstrate in a college setting. Thinking together also prepares students to write in response to various topics presented to them on scholarship applications.

Second, design and share small scholarship campaigns. In our practice, the monthly SchoolWideRead Writing Challenge has become a mainstay in the school communities we serve. Students know when to expect it and how to apply. Teachers, parents, and mentors are notified each month when the challenge is released. They can support students by helping to interpret challenge prompts, reminding them of the due date and encouraging them to enter the competition. And of course, everyone is invited to gather and celebrate the scholarship awardees.

Next, encourage "everyday people" philanthropy to generate scholarship funds and donations. While each family may have limited material resources, offering opportunities for collective giving (ex: crowdfunding/donation box) demonstrates the power of cooperative economics and the community's commitment to education. This also positions a young person's community as an asset, rather than a place from which to escape or an "obstacle to be overcome."

Finally, offer opportunities for sustained support. While traditional scholarships may cover the expense of tuition and room & board, the "extras" that make campus life special are often not included. Community care packages, book drives, and trunk parties can take the burden off a financially strapped household and let a young person know that even though they are "leaving home," the community is always with them.

Do Your Own: Questions to Consider When Starting Your Own Community Supported Scholarship Initiatives:
So you want to create a community supported scholarship campaign? Here are some questions and prompts to help your

family/neighborhood/organization community collective get started:

1. If our young people had more_____, they would know for sure they can attend and navigate college.
2. What is one factor that seems to prevent our students/children from applying to/staying enrolled in the college of their choice?
3. What is one factor that seems to prevent our students/children from applying to and/or winning scholarships?
4. What does each of us have to offer a student in our community as they advance to and through the college experience? (Think time, energy, experience, resources)

We invite you to add your own questions to this list. Whatever you do, don't give up. Continue to build support for your young people as you send them off from community to college with love!

You Can Go to College for FREE!

Sydnie Chandler Monet' Collins

Founder, CEO, and Host of Perfect Timing Podcast, Entrepreneur, Motivational Speaker, and Philanthropist

Sydnie Chandler Monet 'is an award-winning social entrepreneur, podcaster, motivational speaker, and philanthropist, aspiring to have a career through Communications, is a catalyst for change. As a purpose driven influencer, Founder/CEO of Perfect Timing Podcast and Live Your Future Educated – LYFE, at 18 years-old, she is ushering in a new generation of young influencers, celebrities, innovators, and nonprofits by offering a safe platform for them to share their inspiring stories.

Sydnie is a Senior at St. Mary's Ryken High School and President of Student Council, Vice President for Charles County NAACP Youth Council, Save A Girl Save A World Communications Intern and Girls Who Brunch Tour Ambassador.

As a motivational speaker, she provides inspiration to captivate audiences by delivering multi-platform messages at conferences, seminars, and workshops. Sydnie was a guest speaker at the Steve & Marjorie Harvey Foundation "Girls Who Rule The World" Retreat, Girls Who Brunch Tour, and I Believe in Me Summit, where she spoke to over 100 girls about self-esteem, mental health, and entrepreneurship. She kicked-off her "You Are Enough" initiative, asking 100 phenomenal black women to write letters of encouragement for the event and gifted each girl with a gratitude jar! Recently, she raised $7,000 for the #LittleMermaidChallenge which provided 500+ girls with the ability to see themselves on the BIG Screen.

Most notably Sydnie has been named one of only 25 Prudential Emerging Visionaries, LV Media's Best Teen Podcast Award, Maryland Governor's Citation for Outstanding Services to the State, Outstanding Services for GO VAX Ambassador, Maryland Commission for Women Certificate of Recognition and Charles County Women to Watch. Recently featured on Fox 5 DC Good Day, WJLA News 7, NBC News 4, Fox 45 Baltimore, WHUR 96.3 Steve Harvey Morning Show, and The Baltimore Times.

perfecttimingexp@gmail.com | Instagram @perfecttimingpodcast Facebook Perfect Timing Youth Podcast | LinkedIn: Sydnie Collins

Standing Up and Stepping Out

By: Sydnie Chandler Monet' Collins

There was a time when I was extremely timid and I could often be found with my nose smothered in a book. Honestly, I quietly found reading therapeutic and a place of refuge when I didn't have to interact with my peers. I wore funky glasses, had big teeth, and greasy pressed straight hair, all which left me with low self-esteem and confidence. Thankfully, my friends noticed my exchange with the many books I read, and what first felt like I was stranded on a solo island turned into me starting a book club called Live Your Future Educated " –LYFE"! For the first time, I felt like what I cared about mattered. That was the starting point to my leadership and legacy. Unbelievably, an activity that once kept me silent caused me to be dedicated to giving back to my community from elementary and middle school to the present.

I spent much of my teenage years in the performing arts. I surrounded myself in an inclusive environment that embraced my insecurities and allowed me to stand out, even if it meant doing things alone. I recall having 16-18 hour long days that entailed school, the hour and a half it took to get to my five hour dance classes, the hour and a half it took to get home, completing endless homework assignments, etc. Midnight snacks kept me rejuvenated, somehow! However, that rigorous schedule no longer supported my dreams, and my passions shifted. Dance, where I once felt the most comfortable, turned me against my mind and body. I had to ask myself why I was doing this; I had to be honest with myself and God! I desperately needed a change but thought I would be letting my family down; instead, I discovered that we are conditioned to execute the plan established for us at an early age. Understanding my needs and desires were the first step to acknowledging the plan God orchestrated for me. Therefore, I had to prioritize my peace, and dancing was no longer a place of peace for me. Once I understood that, I knew I was on the right path to creating the legacy that I wanted to live. However, this major shift was all happening as senior year was at my doorstep.

Going into my senior year of high school, I underestimated the college and scholarship application processes. Thankfully, I had a strong relationship with God and I had developed good relationships with my instructors, teachers, and my parents, all who often showed me grace as they understood my busy schedule and rigorous workload. Through all of the ups and downs senior year was presenting, I was also being celebrated for showing up and speaking out. In fact, I was chosen as the student speaker at my high school Senior Awards Dinner as President of the Student Council! Amusingly, my high school friends call me Ms. President or Ms. Collins, while administrators affirmed my path by applauding, awarding, and inviting me to use my voice as though I was the house speaker.

Most say I was called, but I say I was chosen. The Bible says in Jeremiah 1:5, "Before I formed you in the womb, I knew you; before you were born, I sanctified you; and I ordained you a prophet to the nations." What does this tell you about the plan that God has for you? For me, it provided security to the struggles I have endured as a teenage change-maker who has been committed to creating a better tomorrow no matter how challenging, demanding, and lonely. The truth is, we don't always know the scope of our trajectory, but there is an opening for us to stand alone in righteousness rather than follow the crowd.

As I adjusted to the reality that not many teens around me think and act like me, I learned to become comfortable with being uncomfortable as a leader. On top of being a dancer, a leader, and applying for college and scholarships, I am also a teen entrepreneur with an award winning international podcast called Perfect Timing, where I have dedicated to giving a voice to Generation Z to inspire confidence, empowerment, and inspiration while simultaneously healing my inner child of self-doubt. Taking on leadership roles and becoming an entrepreneur has meant that I purposefully had to be the odd one out. However, I had grown exhausted from this fact. I was constantly faced with making adult decisions, wanting to be treated like a grown-up and a kid at the same time, and creating a reality that would benefit my future but came with significant sacrifices to my temporary happiness. After the stresses of senior year, I found out I was not alone when I felt like the work would never stop. To counter these attitudes, I learned that one day I will be able to enjoy the fruits of my labor as my work has not been in vain, but all in God's Perfect Timing.

I live by the mantra, "Never fear failure, but be terrified by regret," and it carried me through the majority of my high school years and will continue to do so for the rest of my life. So, when I was faced with imposter syndrome during the college and scholarship application processes suddenly, I did not want to share or discuss all the things that I had done for my community in my essays or interviews. Of course, the whole purpose of applying for scholarships is to be recognized and honored for your academic achievements and community involvement. Conversely, I allowed my efforts to create a better tomorrow for others to pay off, truly realizing it was not about the fear of being singled out, but rather about the benefits of being a leader. Moreover, I learned that forming relationships and being transparent will always reflect the outcome of a favorable situation. Although we live in a very competitive world, leaving little room to live in the moment, I have determined to be intentional and to focus on things that are beneficial to me and with confidence, I implore you to do the same.

As an artist, entrepreneur, daughter, sister, friend, leader, and recent high school graduate, it's inspiring to look back on my darker days and see how I've evolved. I had to be intentional, and I had to ensure that what I was consuming was benefitting my mental health and physical wellbeing. Making drastic changes, balancing pivotal points, and waiting on God's Perfect Timing came with some bumps but much faith and trust. Thankfully, through it all, every experience has become a teachable moment, and I will always be grateful for the lesson. Though I had a late start to my scholarship application process, I have been awarded with over $13,000 in scholarships and will continue to make strides to achieve my higher education goals.

Here's some advice to those of you who are also stepping up and stepping out:

- Fill your cup first and let it run over so you will have enough to give to others.

- Learn that it's okay to be vulnerable.

- Build a report card outlining your interests, passions, dreams, innovations, and accomplishments. There have been times when I didn't trust myself, and the anxiety set in, but I knew if I wanted to be considered for a scholarship or leadership position, I had to show up and believe in myself.

- Build a team of people who will invest in you, a mentor, a life and business coach, and/or a financial, academic, and spiritual advisor.

- Focus on applying for local scholarships in your community, the big ticket scholarships are good, but also exponentially more competitive.
- Having a team with expertise and knowledge will set you up for success.
- Celebrate the work that you are doing (you are your biggest competitor, but also your number one cheerleader).
- Make time for God; He has the perfect path for you. Checking in with His will and way will guarantee and protect your peace.
- Keep the faith!

Orrick R. Quick Sr.

CEO of Oak Tree Publishing
Pastor of New Covenant Church, Entrepreneur,
Motivational Speaker

Orrick R. Quick, Sr. is the proud owner of Oak Tree Publishing LLC. Orrick has devoted his entire life to helping others bring their thoughts and ideas to life whether on stage, in a book or musical album. Oak Tree Publishing has worked with countless authors, speakers and artist to manifest the desired dreams of their clients. Orrick has overcome multiple obstacles in his life such as: two deadly car accidents, (which left him fighting for his life in a coma), physically blind, brain damaged, confined to a body cast for 13 weeks and has learned how to walk over twice before the age of 15 years old. Also, Orrick experienced the devastating event of his mother dying in his arms all at the age of 15 years old. Orrick would then fight through the diagnosis the doctors placed on him as a child. Graduating from North Carolina State University and earning his athletic football scholarship with a bachelor's degree in Sports Management, was one of his greatest achievements. Orrick's mantra is "Never allow your past, to have a meeting with your future, without your potential being present." "Your greatest disappointment in life will not be that you didn't succeed, but that you failed to try."

Orrick Quick was a TV Co-Host for the FOX Daytime talk show, "The Preachers." Orrick Quick was a featured guest on the Dr. Oz show twice and appeared on the television show, "The Real" showcasing his Forever Candles.

Orrick Quick is a trailblazing motivational speaker, life coach and mentor who has been married for 15 years to his lovely wife Ashley. They have 4 children Victoria, Kennedy, Taylor and Orrick Jr.

orrickquick@gmail.com

Sticks and Stones

By: Orrick R. Quick Sr.

We all have been hurt by someone else's words. Words have the power to encourage or discourage. They can either tear you down or build you up. I made the decision many years ago, that I can either allow words to paralyze me or I can use them as fuel to push me! I'll never forget the first time I heard those very words that would somehow push me right into my destiny. "You'll never get a football scholarship." Coming from someone who didn't like me, maybe I should have ignored what they said. However, it was something about those words that cut so deep that I just couldn't ignore them. When my senior year in high school finally arrived, I knew this would be my year. This would be the year I would prove all the doubters wrong. I started the position of middle linebacker as a freshman and was the captain of the defense. In my freshman year, we also went undefeated as well. I had full confidence that this football season would open doors for me to receive my football scholarship.

One day I decided to play a pickup game of basketball. I was always eager to compete, no matter what sport it was. I recognized my brother's car was there as well. As soon as I got out of the car my brother reminded me that I shouldn't be playing basketball with my upcoming football season starting. He reiterated that I should be careful. I told him that I would be okay, and I continued to play basketball. I never knew how much this one day would affect my life. Shortly after the game started, I was guarding a guy and out of nowhere....... SNAP! One of the guys on my team accidentally tripped and fell on the lower part of my leg. I fell to the ground in so much pain. I quickly got back up, trying to convince myself that it wasn't broken. I drove home still trying to convince myself that it wasn't that bad. I went to the doctor and found out that the smaller bone in my calf was broken. I was shattered! How could this happen to me? It was my senior year! I finally healed up completely and joined my teammates with only a few games left in the season. I was so disappointed. Words could not fully describe the feeling that I felt. Watching my teammates receive awards and scholarships that season was one of the hardest things I experienced. What do you do when things do not go as planned? What do you do when life interrupts your dreams? I realize now, that even in that moment of despair I refused to give up. In life, I've discovered that you have to "Declare success with no evidence." You have to convince yourself that things will get better. Confidence is the ability to convince oneself of their capabilities. So, I decided to believe no matter what. Regardless of not receiving a scholarship that year, I did not acquiesce to my situation. I started thinking of other ways of how I could still receive a scholarship. I was told that I could walk on a football team and earn my scholarship that way. So that was exactly what I was going to do. I have learned over the years that when life tries to destroy your plans, create a new one. Just don't ever stop striving until your plans become your reality.

My dream was to play Division 1 football but I had to get accepted into a college so I could transfer to a Division 1 school. So, I called a couple of universities to see what the requirement was for me to walk on their football team. A football recruiting coach gave me their SAT score requirement for acceptance. After receiving their SAT requirement, I immediately got down on my knees to pray and this happened.

Challenging God's Existence

I thank God for my parents Alber O. Quick and Rosetta M. Quick who showed me what trusting in God looked like. They demonstrated that faith in God wasn't just some fairy tale that people talked about. Faith in God was a real thing. I always admired my parents for their boldness. They never hesitated to tell anyone about Jesus Christ and how their lives were transformed through the Gospel. My dad was a Pastor, so I knew one day my time would come to carry on the legacy of faith. Both of my parents had undeniable encounters with God, but now it was my time to have my own. After receiving the SAT requirement from the recruiting coach, I fell to my knees and said, "God, I want to know if you are real or not." I know I was raised in the church, but I want to know if you are real or not. If you're not real and I'm just simply talking to myself then I'm going to choose a different path. So, I am asking for you to help me receive the exact number the recruiting coach gave me. I am not asking for a number below or above; I am asking for the exact number. I need to know if you can pinpoint and give me exactly what I've prayed for. So, I took the SAT the first time and I did not receive the right score. I took the SAT the second time and I still did not receive the right score. I took the SAT for the third and final time of that school year. I finally received the results in the mail. I prayed one more time before I opened the letter. When I saw the results, I dropped my head with disappointment. It was not the number I had prayed for but a lower number. I slumped down on the floor with tears running down my face. I said, "Lord, what happened? Did I not have enough faith? Did I not trust you? Are you real or not?" It crushed my dreams when I saw my score, but all of a sudden while I was sitting on the floor with my knees up to my chest, I heard a voice in the room. This voice said, "Are you finished?"

I replied, "Huh?" The voice said, "Wipe your tears and stand up." I stood up confused after hearing the voice I heard. Then the voice said, "Now go grab all three of your SAT scores and place them on the bed." I did exactly what the voice told me to do. The voice said, "Now you do know that you can combine your two highest scores to receive something called a super score." I said, "Wait a minute, that's right!" Instead of looking at each test score as a whole I could mix and match individual section scores from different test dates. I quickly grabbed a calculator so I could add the two highest scores from different test dates. Whoa! It shocked me! I just stood there in awe! It was the exact number I prayed for! I was speechless! I said, "So you are real?" The voice said, "I am." I was so blown away by what just happened. The voice said, "Do you believe now?" I replied, "Yes." Then God said, "If you would have asked me for more, I would have given it to you, but I wanted to show you that I could pinpoint as you stated before." I was accepted at North Carolina A&T State University. "Aggie Pride!" But my ultimate goal was to play football for a Division 1 University.

One day, while attending class I had a conversation with my instructor. He was also one of the football coaches at A&T State University. He asked me what my plans were concerning school. I told him how I had plans to go to a D1 school as soon as I received enough credits to transfer. This instructor looked me up and down and told me, "Man, you're not going anywhere. You're going to get out here and party like everyone else, you're going to get lost in the shuffle and your grades are going to slip." I was devastated by his comments. I didn't show him that I was upset, but when I got home the tears started to flow. Then all of a sudden God said, "Who determines your success, your instructor or you?" God said, "Prove him wrong." I decided to take what my instructor said to me and use it for fuel. From that day, I was the first person to enter the classroom and the last one to leave. As a result, I ended up transferring from North Carolina A&T University to North Carolina State University on A/B Honor Roll. It was a great feeling to prove to myself that I could accomplish that goal. It felt even better to prove that instructor wrong.

The Scholarship

When I arrived on campus, I knew immediately that this was the University for me, not to mention red is my favorite color. I'll never forget what it felt like when I walked into the football locker room (oh by the way I tried out for the football team and made it). After being on the team for two years my next goal was to earn my scholarship. Then the unimaginable happened. Our head football coach was fired! Even though my last year of football eligibility expired, I still had one more year to graduate. Then all of a sudden, God said "Go ask your head football coach for a scholarship." I replied, "You really want me to ask him for a scholarship after he just got fired?" God replied, "Yes!" So, I called and set up an appointment with him. I walked into his office ready to tell him how much I deserve my scholarship but as I was speaking, he held up his hand for me to stop. He said, "Orrick I know what you have done for this team, and I will make sure you receive your scholarship." To anyone who has ever been discouraged by the negativity of someone's words, whatever you do, don't give up! What the slogan should say is, "Sticks and stones may break my bones, but words really hurt me." I could have given up, all because someone failed to see my vision, but I made a conscious decision to go after my dreams. Always remember, "Never exchange your future expectation for your present situation, and you determine whether your dreams will manifest or not!"

Joseph M. Boumah

Vice President, Heroes & Hearts

Mr. Joseph M. Boumah is Justyn Boumah's father and the Vice-President of Heroes & Hearts. Mr. Boumah is one of our essential culinary workers helping to keep our Las Vegas Strip running stronger. He is a proud graduate of the University of Alabama, where he graduated with a degree in International Relations. Mr. Boumah was born and raised in Central West Africa in Gabon. With his family, he moved to Las Vegas, NV eight years ago. He is a loving father and a dedicated member of the culinary community.

heroesandhearts.org
Instagram & Facebook @heroesandheartslv

A Scholarship Would Have Made a World of Difference:

The Faith of an International Student

By: Joseph Boumah

If I knew then what I know now, my parents, my father in particular, would not have spent thousands and thousands of dollars on my education. Contrarily, I would have told my father that there were ways for me to pursue my education, save money, and earn my degree for free. See, saving money, not wasting money and spending it wisely, was a big thing for my father.

My journey to study in America started when I left Gabon, a small tropical country located in West Africa, and I landed in Tuscaloosa on the campus of the University of Alabama. I quickly understood that as an international student, I would have to pay more than my fellow American students. There was a possibility that I could have gotten away with paying out-of-state tuition, which was less expensive than the international student rate in some cases, but that did not happen so I paid the international student tuition cost for every class from Freshman to Senior year.

During my college years, I did all I knew to do to save my family money. For example, I worked on campus, lived off campus, bought used books, attempted to waive certain fees from my overall tuition bill such as the dining card. However, my efforts did not save my parents very much money. So, I worked diligently on my courses to graduate as quickly as possible in order to help to minimize college costs.

However, I am not alone in my quest for a college eduction in the US. Specifically, there are about 1 Million international students that enroll in US colleges and universities each year. International students are paying approximately $21,000 in yearly tuition to attend school in the US; that's at least $10,000 more than what

American students pay. Consequently, the international student community is choosing to spend more money to study in the United States than what it would cost them to attend college in their own countries. Can you imagine the potential savings if only one third of foreign students were informed, educated and taught how to obtain a scholarship and got the chance to go college debt free or as close to free as possible? The possibilities are truly endless!

As a student I had good grades, but I didn't know I could apply for scholarships. The information about this type of funding was not shared with me and Facebook and all the other social media platforms that we know today were not around when I was in college. Although, this was my story, my own child and other family members will not have the same experience as me, because I found out that college scholarships are available to everyone.

For years I have worked with Dr. Rhee," The Scholarship Doctor" with Scholarship Solutions, and it has been a game changer! I have learned a lot and keep learning every single day about scholarships. Although I cannot change the past, I consistently share with international students, that there are plenty of scholarships available in which they can compete, apply, and qualify. I believe God put me in position to work with, "The Scholarship Doctor" and acquire this knowledge that is positively changing the fate of many international students and their families.

For example, did you know there are states where you can have reduced tuition just because you live in that state or a surrounding state? Therefore, as an international student instead of trying to move where you may have friends and family, you could move to a state where you can take advantage of a program like the Western Undergraduate Exchange (WUE). In some cases, WUE schools, will allow you to pay greatly reduced tuition rates versus the high costs you have at other schools.

Another avenue to help international students save on tuition is by applying to colleges that need you because of your international status. For instance, there are some universities that need to fill their quotas of exchange and international students. Therefore, your international student status gives you an advantage and the opportunity to attend some of the most prestigious universities. This information is so valuable for foreign students and it is tips like this which came from being a part of the Scholarship Solutions program.

Scholarship Solutions has extended services across the United States and internationally. Specifically, the company has served clients in more than 25 states, three continents, and more than 12 countries. Amazingly, I have watched the Scholarship Doctor orient, guide, and direct foreign students and their families just like a movie producer would set all the actors and actresses on stage to create the perfect scene in a movie.

The knowledge that I have acquired while working with her has given me the strength and courage to inform my foreign community that there are options available for them and their loved ones to go to college for free or as close to free as possible. Incredibly, scholarships are for everyone, but students have to be educated and guided on how to secure them.

As mentioned, when I was in college I did not know about all the different little nuggets and ways to get scholarships, have my education paid for, or the path to a free degree. Now, I know better. I want to do better. Dr. Rhee and Scholarship Solutions gave me the platform to help others to save, have the opportunity, and the privilege to earn scholarships. This is something that potentially could change the trajectory of their lives, their family's lives, and the next generation - all for the best.

Now, I have all the knowledge and the tools to get my next degree for free or close to it as possible. But, what about you? Are you ready to do the same? Let Scholarship Solutions and the Scholarship Doctor help you go to college for FREE!

Racquel Watson Boumah

Executive Director, Heroes & Hearts

Mrs. Racquel Watson Boumah is Justyn Boumah's mom. She is the Executive Director of Heroes & Hearts and momanager of Justyn Boumah. Through her family support and kindness, she is able to stay home with Justyn and manage his organizations. Before becoming a momanager, Mrs. Boumah was a business owner in both Las Vegas and Libreville, Gabon. She has two degrees, one in Graphic Design and the other in Moving Graphics. Mrs. Boumah works every day to ensure Heroes & Hearts is everything Justyn wishes.

heroesandhearts.org
Instagram & Facebook @heroesandheartslv

Changing a Legacy

By: Racquel Watson Boumah

"Train up a child in the way he should go; even when he is old he will not depart from it."

Proverbs 22:6 ESV

Lights, Camera, TODDLER! At two years of age my son won his first scholarship! Yes, I did not stutter, he was just two years old! The contest, as scholarships are often referred to for scholars five years old and under, was for residents living in the Las Vegas Valley. The award my son received was simple in nature. It included a certificate, an art kit, and a $25 gift card to Walmart. "WHAT???", you might be thinking, "How does one get college paid for with a certificate, a gift card, and an art kit!?!" Well, it's simple, when my son wins prizes, I consider it a scholarship to me! "Why?", because this means I do not have to buy the things he has won. Therefore, I can save the money I would have used to purchase an item and use it towards college savings or other things. With the gift card, my son was able to pick out and purchase a toy or two for his hard work. Again, a scholarship to me! He gets things he wants, my money goes into college savings, and everyone wins.

At three years old, my son won his first cash based scholarship. He won fourth place in an international photo contest and the prize was 15 BIG BUCKS! The scholarship is called "California Fruit Shoot Contest". To apply for and win this scholarship, my son was tasked with taking a picture of a unique fruit or plant. On a hot Las Vegas day, we went to the park and snapped photos. Guys, it was stressful and the struggle was real!

However, at the end of, " Oh no! Don't drop my camera!" and "I am hot! I want water! I want to swing", we got the picture done and a scholarship win for the books! Although the prize money wasn't enough to pay for a four-year degree at Duke University, one month after winning "Fruit Shoot", my son won a cash award for $150 from another contest and he has continued to win contests and scholarships ever since.

Although my son started winning scholarships at age two, he actually started applying at four months old. As a matter of fact, we have received more "Unfortunately, you didn't win this one." or "Try again next year!" letters than, "Congratulations, you won!". You may be wondering, what was his first scholarship application? I am sure you have heard of it, the Gerber Baby Contest. If not, please google it and tell your friends and family all about it. For Gerber you can be as young as 1 day old and CANNOT be any older than 4 years of age. The Gerber Baby Contest is where my son and I began his scholarship journey and what a journey it has been. You see, being a scholarship winner at any age isn't for the faint of heart nor is it for those who are not willing to persevere with patience, especially if you have a toddler.

Surely as a parent you understand the struggles that comes with raising a child. Getting them to understand right and wrong, how to hold a pencil, or just to sit quietly while you are finishing an email can be challenging. Well, adding scholarships in the middle of an already busy life will test your faith. See, we have delivered contests, scholarship applications, and grants to the post office way past my little man's bedtime. We have recruited the whole family to one page of the scholarship application, drawing paper, or paragraph because it truly takes a village.

Please note, I said "my son and I" and the words "we began"; when applying for scholarships and changing a legacy it isn't an option for a child, at any age, to complete this task on their own. Therefore, if you truly want scholarships to be part of your legacy, you will all need to press in, press through. and press on until the end.

Here are five keys to having "A Multimillion Dollar" scholar:

1. Listen-My daddy used to say, "Eat the chicken and leave the bones." In other words, just take what you need. Long or short car rides are the perfect opportunity to listen to what your toddler or child is saying. Their made up stories and songs could be brilliant for scholarships.

2. Take to Heart-The Bible says "But Mary treasured up all these things, pondering them in her heart." Luke 2:19 ESV As parents, we have the awesome responsibility to raise generations who chart new highways and swim in new rivers. Therefore, our little heartbeats can truly change the world. They just need our hands and hearts to do so.

3. Revisit-When you LISTEN and TAKE TO HEART, the next step is to revisit the chats you had with your little scholar and sort through which projects, concepts, items, songs, or books are truly a passion of his or hers.

4. Put into Action-Once the first three steps are completed, you MUST put them into action. Whether it is writing a book, completing the application, taking the photograph or drawing the picture, putting pen to paper is the step most people have trouble completing. In the words of Nike, "JUST DO IT!"

5. Repeat-Now, that you have the first four pieces in place, you only need to repeat these steps over and over again.

Scholarships, like most anything, are a numbers game. If you apply once you may never see victory. However, if you keep chipping away at the rock, soon it will break in two. My mom says, "If you keep putting the horses in the barn soon they will break out"!

One important nugget we have had throughout our entire scholarship legacy is a little something we like to call," Four Crazy Friends". Everyone needs a village of support or "Four Crazy Friends" who do not mind getting in the trenches when times get tough or you feel discouraged and want to quit. My family is this support system for me and my little guy. When we feel like giving up my sister is not only there to say, "Keep Going! You got this!" but she jumps in the mud with us. My husband is right by my side ready with a drink, snack, and an encouraging word of support and creative flare. My mom is there to assist with lullabies and stories when coloring a picture for a scholarship contest is too stressful for the little guy and his momma! And last, but definitely not least, my little guy himself shows up every time. Amazingly, he places his little hand on my shoulder, uses his little voice to say thank you, and his hugs and kisses make all the difference in the world.

Naya Rivera once wrote, "Butterflies can't see the color of their wings but we as humans can see how beautiful they are. Likewise, you might not think you are good enough but others can see how special and amazing you are". So, find your" Four Crazy Friends" support system, so when times get tough they will be there to guide, encourage, and lead your child and you. The world is waiting and watching so show them, in the words of my son, "You don't have to be BIG or STRONG to do BIG things." Trust the process through to the promised land and together you all can change your legacy.

Use the space below to list three-five people you consider your "Four Crazy Friends". Add their names, phone numbers, and email addresses:

1.

2.

3.

4.

5.

Here is a short scholarship list for children five years and under:

- Sodexo STOP Hunger Scholarship (Ages 5 - 25)
- PBS Writing Contest (Grades K - 5)
- Dover Coloring Contest (All Ages)
- Gerber Baby Contest (Ages 0 - 4)
- Debbie Dreams (Grades K - 12)
- Fruit Shoot (All Ages)

You Can Go to College for FREE!

Justyn D Boumah

CEO & Founder, Heroes & Hearts

Mr. Justyn D. Boumah is the 8-year-old CEO and Founder of the 501c3 organization, Heroes & Hearts. Justyn is a social entrepreneur and an award-winning author who has been recognized internationally by public figures such as Prince Harry and Meghan Markle. He has been featured on the TODAY Show, NBC Nightly News with Lester Holt: Kids Edition, People Magazine TV, ABC World News, and as Newsmax's Patriot of the Week for his young ingenuity and purity of heart. Incredibly, Justyn has five annual giveback events ~ The Blessing Project, Art & Reading, Learning is Fun Libraries, STEM Days: Robotics, Bricks, and Kicks, and Super Justyn's Giveaway, where he has touched 100s of lives. Please see his website and follow us on social media so that you can know all of what Justyn is doing to change the world.

heroesandhearts.org
Instagram & Facebook @heroesandheartslv

The 5 Sweet Nuggets to Applying for Scholarships

By: Justyn D. Boumah

Hello! My name is Justyn and I am eight years of age. I have done a lot of things like, I have been on a championship baseball team, published books, did a TEDx talk in Apex, NC, where I will be Mayor one day, started a non profit organization called Heroes & Hearts, traveled to 12 countries including Poland to help kids from Ukraine, learned my multiplication facts up to 12, had my picture on the big screen in Times Square, and I have won lots of scholarships!

Did you know little kids can apply for scholarships just like big kids and adults? I apply for scholarships and other contests where I win money and prizes! Recently, I was so excited because I got a Starbucks gift card. When I get money, sometimes they give me a big check. But, you can't put the check in the bank; it's only so you can take fun pictures.

When I met Daymond John from Shark Tank, it was because I entered a business pitch competition. Although I didn't win, I got tickets to the award show. Mr. John autographed his children's book for me, and I got to do one of my favorite things, ride on an airplane!

My mom and aunty say scholarships come in all kinds of ways and I think I'm starting to understand what they mean. For example, I love baseball and because I won a contest, I got tickets to see the Arizona Diamondbacks in their ginormous stadium! Just last week I won my biggest scholarship ever! I get $10,000, a trip to Los Angeles, a day at Disneyland, and I get to fly on Delta Airlines which has free movies and free snacks!

I think everyone should apply for scholarships. You can win money, prizes, trips, and gift cards. I don't know where I am going to college yet but I have lots of scholarships to help pay for it. Guess how much?!?! Over $40,000 in scholarships, grants, and prizes!

To help you on your scholarship quest I wanted to give you five sweet nuggets to applying for scholarships. Follow these nuggets and I know you can win scholarships just like me!

1. You Must Apply!

    Applying is the first step to winning any scholarship. Before applying you have to prepare. I prepare for each scholarship contest by gathering my gadgets. My scholarship gadgets include pens, pencils, paper, crayons, color pencils, and notebooks. These gadgets help me to win scholarships!

2. You Need Lots of Snacks, Especially Cookies and Chicken Fingers!

    In order to get through writing essays, taking pictures, or drawing a picture, snacks are required. Snacks are an essential part of keeping your mind sharp, your spirit awake, your bellies full, and your muscles strong! It is important to honor those yummy treats who gave up their lives so people can have something to eat while applying for scholarships.

3. Use Your Kuumba!

    Kuumba is creativity in Swahili. When you use creativity the judges will love it! Creativity can determine if you are the winner or not the winner.

    Here are a few ways you can be creative and use your kuumba when applying for scholarships.

- A. Use lots of color. It's all about the color when talking about scholarships for kids. The judges think color is king or queen!
- B. Be unique. By using language skills, inspiring quotes or sayings, or by telling a story, it shows you're unique.
- C. Be Kind. I say, "'Kindness is like fire, when you spread it, it grows and grows!" When you are kind, people will help you. For my scholarships I have interviewed people, asked my friends to be in videos with me, and asked my family to help me on a creative project. Because I was kind, they said YES!

4. Believe in yourself! You must believe you can win. I'm going to tell you, don't ask, "what ifs". The "what ifs" will effect your essay and your confidence to win your scholarship. So if your mind tells you, "What if my sentence is incorrect?" You tell your mind, "My sentence is correct and the judges are going to love it!" When you believe and create, you are a winner!

5. Keep Applying, You Might Not Get it on the First Try.

    It might seem hard to apply for a scholarship at first and you may not win on your first try but mommy says, "We win or learn.", so just keep applying. Also, ask a parent to help you on your scholarship journey. Oh! And here are a few other important nuggets when you apply.

    - A. Review and take note of the deadline. The deadline means the scholarship has ended and you can't apply for it anymore. Deadlines are very important and you should never ignore them.
    - B. When you apply, make sure to read all the rules. If you can't read ask your parent to help you. I ask my Mommy,

Daddy, Aunty, and Grandmier (that's Grandmother in French) for help all the time with my scholarships.

C. The last and final step is to submit. When you finish your essay, story, or drawing you must submit. This is the only way the judges know you have applied.

Wow! You did it! Now you will be a scholarship winner just like me! I'm excited for us to say, "We're going to the Championship! We're going to the Championship! Which one? The Scholarship Championship of course! You got this scholarship winner! Bye!

Scholarships

Scholarship Name: American Legion National High School Oratorical Contest
Website: legion.org/scholarships/oratorical
General Information: The oratorical contest is open to students under the age of 20. A complete list of topics are available online. Please see their website for additional details.

Scholarship Name: American Road & Transportation Builders
Website: artbatdf.org
General Information: Contest is open to students in elementary school through graduate school. Contestant must submit a video on transportation infrastructure. Visit the website for more details.

Scholarship Name: Apprentice Ecologist Initiative Youth Scholarship Program
Website: wildernessproject.org/volunteer_apprentice_ecologist.php
General Information: Scholarships are open to students between the ages of 13 and 21 and can be from any country around the world. Visit their website for additional details.

Scholarship Name: Atlas Shrugged Essay Contest
Website: aynrand.org/students/essay-contests/atlas-shrugged
General Information: This scholarship is available to high school, undergraduate and graduate students. Please see their website for additional details.

Scholarship Name: Autism Scholarship
Website: dbphoenixcriminallawyer.com/autism-scholarship
General Information: This scholarship is open to a US citizens who have been diagnosed with ASD (DSM-V). Please see their website for additional details.

Scholarship Name: Ben Carson Scholarship
Website: carsonscholars.org
General Information: The Carson Scholars Fund awards college scholarships to students in grades 4 through 11 who excel academically and are dedicated to serving their communities. Visit the website for more details.

Scholarship Name: CBC Spouses Education Scholarship
Website: cbcfinc.org
General Information: Applicants must be U.S. citizens or permanent residents, have a minimum 2.5 GPA, be enrolled full-time in an accredited academic institution, and reside in a district represented by a member of the Congressional Black Caucus. Visit the website for more details.

Scholarship Name: Debbie's Dream Scholarship
Website: debbiesdream.org
General Information: Contest is open to high school, middle school, and elementary school students across the United States. Students are provided an essay prompt to explore how they would help make a difference for stomach cancer patients. Visit the website for more details.

Scholarship Name: Driven Coffee Scholarship
Website: drivencoffee.com/scholarship
General Information: This scholarship is available to undergraduate students. Students must write three short essays. Please see their website for additional details.

Scholarship Name: Don't Text and Drive Scholarship
Website: digitalresponsibility.org
General Information: Scholarship is open to grades 9-12 and college/ graduate students. Visit the website for more details.

Scholarship Name: EK Insurance Scholarship
Website: ekinsurance.com/scholarship.htm
General Information: The scholarship is for undergraduate and graduate students. Students must submit a video on a topic related to insurance. Please see their website for additional details.

Scholarship Name: Elks Scholarship
Website: elks.org
General Information: Current high school seniors, or the equivalent, who are citizens of the United States are eligible to apply. Visit the website for more details.

Scholarship Name: Engineer Girl Essay Contest
Website: engineergirl.org
General Information: Write about a unique topic regarding engineering. Contest is open to individual girls and boys, ages 8 – 18, in each of three categories based on grade level. Visit the website for more details.

Scholarship Name: Financial Goals Scholarship
Website: 1fbusascholarship.com/Award
General Information: This scholarship is available to students ages 18 years and older. Students must submit a 500 word essay. Please see their website for additional details.

Scholarship Name: Gen and Kelly Tanabe Scholarship
Website: genkellyscholarship.com
General Information: Scholarship is open to students in grades 9-12, college, or graduate school students who are legal U.S. residents. Applicant must submit an essay answering why they deserve the scholar- ship or their academic or career goals. Visit the website for more details.

Scholarship Name: Jack Kent Cooke Foundation Scholarship
Website: jkcf.org
General Information: Award is open to elementary through college students. Visit the website for more details.

Scholarship Name: Maryknoll Student Essay Contest
Website: maryknollsociety.org
General Information: Contest is open to students enrolled in grades 6-12. Applicant must submit an essay on the topic: "Sharing Good News." Visit the website for more details.

Scholarship Name: Minecraft Scholarship
Website: apexminecrafthosting.com/minecraft-scholarship
General Information: The scholarship is for high school and

college students. Visit their website for additional details.

Scholarship Name: Notorious RBG Women of Tomorrow Scholarship
Website: nshss.org/scholarships/s/notorious-rbg-women-of- tomorrow-scholarship
General Information: The scholarship is available to rising high school freshman to incoming college freshman. Students must submit an essay of between 500 - 800 words Female students are strongly encouraged to apply, however it is open to male students as well. Please see their website for additional details.

Scholarship Name: Raftelis Leadership Scholarship
Website: raftelis.com/who-we-are/giving-back
General Information: The Raftelis Leadership Scholarship is open to junior and seniors in college as well as graduate students. They seek students who are motivated and well rounded. Please see their website for additional details.

Scholarship Name: SMART Scholarship
Website: smartscholarship.org/smart
General Information: Scholarship is open to students age 18 and over who are STEM majors. Must have 1.5 years left on your degree. Visit the website for more details.

Scholarship Name: Technology Addiction Awareness Scholarship
Website: digitalresponsibility.org/technology-addiction-awareness-scholarship

General Information: This scholarship is available to high school, undergraduate, and graduate students. Students must create a 140 character (not words) essay. Please see their website for additional details.

Scholarship Name: The Beacon Scholarship for Rural America
Website: carrot-top.com/beacon-scholarship
General Information: The Beacon Scholarship for Rural America provides financial assistance for college to residents of rural areas. Please see their website for additional details.

Scholarship Name: The Ike Foundation Scholarship
Website: theikefoundation.org/get-involved/college-scholarship-program/
General Information: The scholarship is for graduating high school seniors. Special consideration is given to those who demonstrate service to the fishing or conservation world. Please see their website for additional details.

Scholarship Name: Tylenol Undergraduate Scholarships
Website: tylenol.com/scholarship
General Information: Annual awards for graduate students, who are interested in the healthcare field. Award is based on leadership responsibilities in community and school activities. Visit the website for more details.

Scholarship Name: Union Plus Scholarship
Website: unionplus.org/benefits/education/union-plus-scholarships
General Information: The scholarship is for high school seniors, undergraduate, and graduate students. You, your spouse, or dependent must be a current or retired member of a participating union. Please see their website for additional details.

Scholarship Name: Veterans of Foreign Wars Scholarship
Website: vfw.org/Community
General Information: The essay contest encourages young minds grades 6-8 to examine America's history, along with their own experiences in modern American society, by drafting a 300- to 400-word essay, expressing their views based on a patriotic theme chosen by the VFW Commander-in-Chief. Visit the website for more details.

Scholarship Name: We the Future Contest
Website: constitutingamerica.org
General Information: Contest is open to kindergarten through graduate/professional school, adults 25 years of age and older, and seniors 65 years of age and older. Visit the website for more details.

Scholarship Name: Wells Fargo Veterans Scholarship
Website: learnmore.scholarsapply.org/wellsfargoveterans
General Information: This scholarship is for veterans of the U.S. Armed Services and spouses or widows of disabled

service members. The scholarship can be used for certification or traditional university programs. Visit the website for more details.

Scholarship Name: Whitaker Foundation Art Scholarship
Website: whitakerwatercolors.org/the-foundation-scholarship-fund-and-application/
General Information: The Whitaker Foundation Art Scholarship is open to currently enrolled undergraduates. Students seeking a bachelor's degree in either fine art with an emphasis on watercolor or museum studies and art history are encouraged to apply.

Scholarship Name: Youth on Course Scholarship
Website: youthoncourse.org/college-scholarships
General Information: Scholarship is for high school seniors who have been involved in golf but its open to those interested in golf, too. Visit the website for more details.

Scholarship Name: ZNEF Scholarship Program
Website: znef.org/znef-scholarships
General Information: Scholarship is open to high school seniors and college students. Visit the website for more details.

Thanks and Tips

RHEA M. WATSON - First, thank you to my Lord and Savior Jesus Christ, My Dear Heavenly Father, and Precious Holy Spirit, you continue to lead and direct me. I will always follow you. Collaborating Authors and Pastor Quick - We did it! Thank you for your support, trust, and kinship. We are #1 Best Sellers! Mama, you are the editing queen; the book is stellar! Thank you for always being my biggest cheerleader and fan! Family, Followers, Fans, Clients, Mentors, Word of Life, Scholarship Solutions Staff, Purchasers, and Readers - You're the BEST! Much love and thanks for supporting.

Tips:

- amvets.org/scholarships
- geteducated.com
- heismanscholarship.com
- vfw.org/community/youth-and-education
- americancollegefoundation.org

***

LILI ST. CHRISTOPHER - Special thanks to my husband, Lorne Sr., who has provided a runway for our children to take off and to have a safe place to land. To my heart, Lorne II, and my soul, Laila Faith – the sky is the limit when you keep God in it. To my parents, Pastor Carl Prude, Sr., and Dr. Lillie B. Lewis Prude - Hallelujah! It's the highest praise To the members of the College Bound Village (CBV) family - you inspire me to walk daily in Confidence, Blessings and Victory (CBV). Be encouraged and Let's Get This Money for College!

MARILYN GILBERT - MITCHELL - Thank you to my late sister, Charlotte, who said, "Show em who and whose you are." Great gratitude goes to my mother, Eunice Gilbert, a 50-year educator; Aunt Bettie; mentors, Dr BJ Bolden & Dr. William Harris; daughters & granddaughter, Amber, Joi, & Violet; cousin, Jessica; Sistahs (Tricey & Kae); brother, Rod; 7-Phi from Tuskegee Univ. (GB, CB, WF, CJ, FR, & RW); & those who prayed for me, shared my information, supported MGM College Services LLC, and purchased my services.

Tips:

1) NCAN - National College Attainment Network (ncan.org)
2) NACAC - National Association for College Admission Counseling (nacacnet.org)
3) UNCF - United Negro College Fund
4) Reach Higher (reachhigher.org)
5) College Scorecard - from the U Dept. of Education (collegescorecard.ed.gov)
6) ISAC - Illinois Student Assistance Commission (isac.org)
7) Big Future from College Board (bigfuture.collegeboard.org)

***

CAROL BEN - DAVIES - I would like to express my sincerest gratitude to my parents, Eric and Dolly Ben-Davies, for their unwavering support, prayers, encouragement, and belief in everything I attempt to achieve. Your love and guidance have been my foundation throughout my life. I'm so proud to add my own book to our family book collection! To the love of my life,

Ken, your unwavering support and love have been evidence of answered prayers. Thank you for believing in me, pushing me to write, grow a business and for being my rock. To my Sweet Ks, Kennedy and Kristen, you are my greatest joy, love and motivation. To my sisters Maureen and Tricia, thank you for always cheering me on and being there for me. To The Crew - your friendship and unwavering belief in my abilities have been a true blessing in my life. My In-Loves, nieces, nephews, cousins, aunts & uncles, thank you for instilling the importance of family, faith and fortitude. To everyone who has ever supported me, Thank you!

***

SHYMIKA STEPHENSON - DAVISON - I would like to thank God for making all things possible, my family and friends, especially my husband, son, and sisters for their support, and the Precollege Solutions Family for every student, family, tutoring company, and nonprofit, we have been able to work beside. Thank you!

Tips:

- Grad Resources - For Graduate Students: precollegesolutions.com/gradresources

- College Board - SAT, AP, College Search and Admission Tools — Test Information: collegeboard.org

- College and Career Readiness | ACT- Test Information: act.org

NATHAN McCALLA - Thank you Jesus for showing me I was worth the price you paid on the cross. Nothing compares to the peace, freedom, and certainty in surrendering my life to you. And thank you to everyone who has encouraged, inspired, and supported me throughout the journey - my wife, mom, dad, grandparents, cousins, aunts, uncles, good friends, teachers, mentors, and coaches. Your impact on me has, without a doubt, shaped me into the person who I am today. Thank you all so, so much.

***

NIKAYLA WILLIAMS - Thank you, God for being my guiding light and saving grace; Parents, family, friends, and mentors for being an incredible, unwavering and loving support system; Scholarship Doctor, Dr. Rhea Watson, for being a catalyst in my life, professionally and personally; And you, reader, for your trust.

***

ZENA ROBINSON-WOUADJOU - I am expressing love and deep gratitude for my parents, Frank (Adu) Robinson and Claretha Fleming-Robinson, for instilling a love of learning and commitment to community. I am grateful to be the mother of two beautiful human beings, Abdullaye & Kalimah Wouadjou, who inspire and challenge me to be greater. SchoolWideRead thanks the young people, families, and school communities who allow us to work and build with them, as well as the educators who came before us and those to come.

Tips:

- The ScholarPrep Nation offers an "Afrocentric College & Life Access Platform as well as the ScholarPre Organizer to help students and families prepare for the college journey and admissions process. IG: scholarprepnation

***

SYDNIE CHANDLER MONET' COLLINS - Thank you so much Ms. Rhea Watson for being a catalyst to sharing my story in such a beautiful way, this book will help so many and is a true blessing. Thank you to my mom for the late nights, Uncle Tracy for the listening ear, Aunt Meme, Tayone, Ms. Cidra Sebastien, Ms. Glenda Gill, Dad, General Birckhead, Aunt Vanessa, and other friends and family for your constant support. My success is a result of your love and trust in me.

***

JOSEPH M. BOUMAH - All my steps are ordered by Him so thank you God. I would like to thank my parents for trusting and investing in me. I would like to thank all the educators who I have encountered so far in my journey, especially Dr. Rhee who inspires me and shows me what it takes to succeed in the academic world. I would like to express my gratitude to all my co-authors for being mentioned among them. Last and not least, I would like to thank my wife and my son for being the driving force behind everything I do.

***

RACQUEL WATSON BOUMAH - Thank you to my husband Joseph and my son Justyn. You both are the joy of my life and I love you tremendously and always. Thank you sister, the Scholarship Doctor, I love you. I am thankful you created a platform where I can share with parents how they can help their little ones with the scholarship process.

JUSTYN BOUMAH - I want to thank my family in Africa, North America, and Europe for everything you do for me. I want to thank Jesus for saving me. I want to thank God and Holy Spirit for helping me. Thanks to my Pastors and KMU Ministers for all they do for kids like me at church. I also want to thank Jelly Belly for having the best jelly beans and McDonald's, Cane's, and In-n-Out for the yummy food that kept me full, especially when writing my chapter!

Rhea's Resources

The Three Cs

One of the most important ways to going to college for free is by being involved with community service. When it comes to community service, think about things you enjoy and remember these important Cs.

- Creativity
- Consistency
- Community

Also, use these resources to find fantastic places to volunteer: You can contact 211 or visit volunteermatch.org. These resources are available to anyone throughout the United States and beyond.

Furthermore, it is important to track your volunteer hours. Using a spreadsheet or document to log your duties, responsibilities, and tasks will help you in your quest of going to college for free. On your volunteer tracking worksheet include some of the following things:

- Date
- Event Location
- Activities
- Start time
- End time
- Total hours served
- Duties
- Supervisor/Coordinator

Keeping tack of this information each time you volunteer will help you when completing your scholarship and college applications. Do your best to keep your volunteer service current. You will be so happy when you have an up-to-date record of all that you have done in the community.

Slaying Your Scholarship Application

When applying for scholarships it is paramount that your application is stellar, stands out, and helps you to slay the scholarship! Therefore, when you complete your scholarship applications (and essays), you must use correct grammar and spelling. If you have problems in these areas, ask your Scholarship Coach, Parent, Advisor, Mentor, and/or Counselor to look at your documents. Have them proofread your materials to insure that you are presenting yourself in the best light possible on any applications or essays.

You may have heard it from the North, South, East, and West, but I am here to reiterate what you have been told. When applying for scholarships and colleges you must clean up your social media images and pages. Believe it or not, scholarship and college programs search your social media platforms. They want to "investigate" your true character and trust that what you show the world through media is who you are or hope to be. So, do not have or post questionable photos, text, or videos. Be watchful of what is posted on your social media pages by others. Honestly, your "connections and associations" could reflect negatively on you. Social media can make or break you in the scholarship, college, and career worlds. Do not give anyone any reason to pass you over for a scholarship. So make your social platforms reflective of the applications you are submitting to scholarships and colleges. In addition to the above information consider these points as well:

- Is your username offensive?
- Are you sharing a grandiose lifestyle?
- Are you adding value?
- Are you in groups that reflect positivity?

Presentation is key when slaying your scholarship application and although many applications are electronic they sometimes still require specific uploads. Of course, when applications must be mailed in, you want them look the best possible. Therefore, when submitting your applications online or through the mail, consider these things.

- If you are mailing your applications, print it on nice paper.
- Have a professional photograph, a headshot or senior/graduation picture works exceptionally well.
- Include a copy of your resume. This will allow the readers to get to know more about you.
- Mail your application in a 9 x 11 envelope. Do not destroy your hard work by folding your application. Keep it nice and pristine.
- Pay extra to mail your application so that it will arrive in one - three days, guaranteed.

Remember you are asking for 1000s of dollars in FREE MONEY, and many times from major corporations and organizations. Think about how your application should look if you want to secure that kind of money. Also, since scholarships are hundreds to thousands of dollars, be prepared to spend a lot of quality time on your applications, at least five hours on each one. Treat the application process like a part time job and when doing so you could possibly create a pathway where you can go to college for FREE.

Check out these sample scholarship documents that will help you to be prepared for your scholarship and college application processes.

You Can Go to College for FREE!

Sample Scholarship Application

Full Name:
_____

Complete Home Address:
_____
_____

Cell Phone:
_____

Email Address:
_____

Unweighted GPA
_____

Weighted GPA:
_____

Test Scores and Dates:
_____
_____
_____
_____

You Can Go to College for FREE!

Graduation Date:
_____

List the names of five (5) references. Explain your relationship to the references:
_____
_____
_____
_____
_____

You Can Go to College for FREE!

Sample Resume

Your Name

---

111 Your Place Las Vegas, NV 12340 | youremail@email.com 555-555-5555

OBJECTIVE To obtain a merit baed scholarship to further my education, advance my skills, and increase my knowledge in the areas of human relations, finance, and business.

EDUCATION Desert Spruce High School
Los Angeles, CA
Valley College
Las Vegas, NM

EXPERIENCE
April 2022- Shed Manager
Present   Serving Services
Director of sanitation, management of monetary funds, supervising checks and balances of finances and protect of relationships with business partners and colleagues.

July 2020- Sales Representative
March 2022 Back Row Sports
Representative of sports products and memorabilia, supervising checks and balances of finances and displaying the high quality of customer service.

January 2019-Cashier/Clerk
June 2020   Taco Tell
Representative for food services, management of monetary funds supervising checks and balances of finances.

VOLUNTEER EXPERIENCE

January 2018- Apprentice
Present   KKTU Television Station
Director for inspirational television programs which promoted healthy lifestyles for different age and ethnic groups.

January 2018- Youth Choir/Usher
Present   Greater C.M.E. Church
Involved with all aspects of the choir and the usher board including community outreach to the homeless

January 2017- Dancer
June 2018   Dance Dynamics
Creative expressions through dance and music for youth, senior, and various community organizations.

January 2015- Mentor
June 2017   Soul to Soul
Taught creative expressions through dance and music in a community center geared toward ethnic youth.

SKILLS *Microsoft and Apple
　　　　*App Development
　　　　*Conversational French

ACTIVITIES *Student Government Association
　　　　*Science Club
　　　　*Varsity Golf

AWARDS 　*Outstanding Student-Kappa Alpha Alumni
　　　　*Parks and Recreation-Golf Award
　　　　*Spirit of Excellence Award

You Can Go to College for FREE!

Sample Scholarship Essay Question

In 500 words or less, please describe your educational goals and how receiving this scholarship will help you continue your education: (Always Type Your Final Draft)

First Draft

You Can Go to College for FREE!

You Can Go to College for FREE!

You Can Go to College for FREE!

You Can Go to College for FREE!

You Can Go to College for FREE!

Second Draft

You Can Go to College for FREE!

You Can Go to College for FREE!

You Can Go to College for FREE!

You Can Go to College for FREE!

You Can Go to College for FREE!

You Can Go to College for FREE!

Third Draft

You Can Go to College for FREE!

You Can Go to College for FREE!

You Can Go to College for FREE!

You Can Go to College for FREE!

You Can Go to College for FREE!

Notes

You Can Go to College for FREE!